MATT AND TOM OLDFIELD

ULTIMATE
FOOTBALL HEROES

DE BRUYNE

FROM THE PLAYGROUND
TO THE PITCH

DINO

Published by Dino Books
an imprint of John Blake Publishing
2.25, The Plaza,
535 Kings Road,
Chelsea Harbour
London, SW10 0SZ

www.johnblakepublishing.co.uk

www.facebook.com/johnblakebooks 🇫
twitter.com/jblakebooks 🇹

This edition published in 2018

ISBN: 978 1 78946 005 6

British Library Cataloguing-in-Publication Data:

A catalogue record for this book is available from the British Library.

Design by www.envydesign.co.uk

Printed and bound in Great Britain by Clays Ltd, Elcograf S.p.A.

1 3 5 7 9 10 8 6 4 2

Papers used by John Blake Publishing are natural, recyclable products made from
wood grown in sustainable forests. The manufacturing processes conform to the
environmental regulations of the country of origin.

Every attempt has been made to contact the relevant copyright-holders, but some
were unobtainable. We would be grateful if the appropriate people could contact us.

John Blake Publishing is an imprint of Bonnier Publishing.
www.bonnierpublishing.co.uk

For Noah and Nico,
Southampton's future strikeforce

ULTIMATE
FOOTBALL HEROES

Matt Oldfield is an accomplished writer and the editor-in-chief of football review site *Of Pitch & Page*. Tom Oldfield is a freelance sports writer and the author of biographies on Cristiano Ronaldo, Arsène Wenger and Rafael Nadal.

Cover illustration by Dan Leydon.
To learn more about Dan visit danleydon.com
To purchase his artwork visit etsy.com/shop/footynews
Or just follow him on Twitter @danleydon

TABLE OF CONTENTS

ACKNOWLEDGEMENTS

First of all, I'd like to thank John Blake Publishing –
and particularly my editor James Hodgkinson – for
giving me the opportunity to work on these books
and for supporting me throughout. Writing stories for
the next generation of football fans is both an honour
and a pleasure.

I wouldn't be doing this if it wasn't for my brother
Tom. I owe him so much and I'm very grateful for
his belief in me as an author. I feel like Robin setting
out on a solo career after a great partnership with
Batman. I hope I do him (Tom, not Batman) justice
with these new books.

Next up, I want to thank my friends for keeping

me sane during long hours in front of the laptop. Pang, Will, Mills, Doug, John, Charlie – the laughs and the cups of coffee are always appreciated.

I've already thanked my brother but I'm also very grateful to the rest of my family, especially Melissa, Noah and of course Mum and Dad. To my parents, I owe my biggest passions: football and books. They're a real inspiration for everything I do.

Finally, I couldn't have done this without Iona's encouragement and understanding during long, work-filled weekends. Much love to you.

CHAPTER 1

MANCHESTER CITY'S MAIN MAN

Stamford Bridge, 30 September 2017

There was great excitement all across the footballing world, but especially around the Stamford Bridge stadium in West London. It was a sell-out for the biggest game of the Premier League season so far – the champions, Chelsea, versus the most entertaining team in England, Manchester City.

So, who would win the battle of the best? Which manager would come out on top: Chelsea's Antonio Conte or City's Pep Guardiola? And which brilliant Belgian would shine the brightest: Chelsea's Eden Hazard or City's midfield maestro, Kevin De Bruyne?

For Kevin, the match meant more than just another three points for his team. Back in 2012, at the age of twenty, he had made the bold move from his Belgian club Genk to Chelsea, with high hopes of becoming 'the next Frank Lampard', or even 'the new Zinedine Zidane'.

Kevin's manager at Chelsea, José Mourinho, had promised him game-time but, instead, he spent two seasons either out on loan, or sitting on the bench. Kevin had always been a stubborn star. He was impatient and strong-willed too. When he saw that he had no chance at Chelsea, he decided to make a name for himself somewhere else. He went to Germany and quickly became 'The King of the Assists' at VfL Wolfsburg.

Now, Kevin was back in England, starring for a new club. He was the best player in the Premier League and Manchester City were the best team too. Kevin had no hard feelings towards his old club but nevertheless, he had a point to prove to some people. It was time to show, once and for all, that he wasn't a 'Chelsea flop'. Five years on, Kevin was a completely different playmaker – older, wiser, and a whole lot better.

'Let's win this, lads!' his captain David Silva clapped and cheered before kick-off.

That wouldn't be easy away at Stamford Bridge, but City were top of the table and playing with so much style and confidence. With Kevin starting every attack in central midfield, Pep's grand plan was working brilliantly. City had thrashed Liverpool 5–0, then Watford 6–0, then Crystal Palace 5–0. Could they thrash Chelsea too?

Kevin dropped deep to get the ball as often as possible. He had two fantastic feet, capable of creating magic. Sometimes, he curled beautiful long passes over the top for City's speedy winger Raheem Sterling to chase. Sometimes, he played clever one-twos with Raheem, David and right-back Kyle Walker. Sometimes he was on the right, sometimes he was on the left, and sometimes he was in the middle. Kevin was everywhere, doing everything to help his team to win.

His first chance to score came from a free kick. He had scored plenty in his career, even one against

Barcelona in the Champions League. This time, however, his Belgian international teammate Thibaut Courtois made a comfortable save.

'Aaaaaaaaaahhhhhhhhh,' the City fans let out a groan of disappointment, like the air escaping from a balloon. Kevin was so talented that they expected him to get it right every time.

'Next time,' he thought to himself as he ran back into position. As the game went on, Kevin, and City, got better and better.

CHANCE! Kevin crossed to Gabriel Jesus but it was intercepted by a Chelsea defender.

CHANCE! Kevin delivered a dangerous corner kick but Gabriel headed wide.

CHANCE! Kevin chipped the ball towards Gabriel but he headed wide again.

The City fans were growing restless in their seats. Their team was creating lots and lots of chances – but without their star striker, Sergio Agüero, who was going to step up and score the winning goal?

Playing in his new deeper midfield role, Kevin hadn't scored yet that season. Pep wanted him to be the team's pass-master, using his amazing X-ray vision to set up goals for other players. But what if they couldn't score?

Kevin could strike a brilliant shot, full of power and swerve. Like his hero Zidane, he was the complete midfielder, and he was determined to prove himself as a big game player. A win against Chelsea would keep City top of the Premier League, above their local rivals, Manchester United. His team needed him more than ever...

'Attack!' Pep shouted from the sidelines. 'Attack!'

So, the next time that Kevin played a quick pass to Gabriel, he kept running forward for the one-two. Kevin got the ball back and burst through the Chelsea midfield. He was just outside the penalty area now, with plenty of space to...

'Shoot!' the City fans urged. 'Shoot!'

It was on his left foot but Kevin didn't really have a weaker foot, just two magic wands. He steadied himself, pulled his leg back and struck the ball sweetly. *Abracadabra!* It flew through the air and over Courtois's outstretched arms.

Goooooooooooooooooooaaaaaaaaaaaaaaaaallllllllllll llllllllllllll!!!!!!!!!!!!!!!!!!!!

'DE BRUYNE!!' the TV commentator cried out. 'Oh, that's special!'

What an important goal! As the ball hit the back of the net, the City supporters went wild. Kevin ran towards them, shaking his finger and roaring like a lion. He was so pumped up with pride and joy. He wanted to win the Premier League title so much.

On the touchline, Pep punched the air with delight. Their Brazilian substitute Danilo couldn't contain his excitement. He ran straight onto the pitch to bump chests with their hero. Soon, Kevin was at the centre of a big team hug.

'Come on!' he called out to the supporters and, in reply, they sang their favourite song:

Ohhhhhhhh! Kevin De Bruyne!

Ohhhhhhhh! Kevin De Bruyne!

It was an amazing moment for Manchester City's main man, one that he would never forget. Kevin had scored his team's winning goal, and against Chelsea! It didn't get any better than that. Back at

Stamford Bridge, the Belgian had showed the world that he was now a superstar.

'Kev, you're the best!' his manager Pep Guardiola said with a huge smile on his face.

Mourinho might not have believed in him at Chelsea, but Guardiola certainly did at Manchester City. And most importantly, Kevin believed in himself. He had always known that he had the talent, the drive and the resilience to reach the very top, even during his early days in Drongen.

CHAPTER 2

DRONGEN DAYS

The De Bruynes really loved football. Anna had first discovered the beautiful game when she was a young girl, living with her family in London. Her husband, Herwig, shared her passion. He had spent years playing for teams in Belgium's lower leagues. So as soon as their son, Kevin, was old enough to walk, they couldn't wait to introduce him to their favourite sport.

When they dropped a small football at his feet, Kevin soon worked out what to do with it.

KICK! His little leg shot forward and the ball rolled slowly across the living room carpet.

'Yes, that's it!' His parents clapped and cheered.

Kevin copied their clapping. This was fun! He wanted another go.

KICK! The ball rolled more quickly this time, through the doorway and out into the hall.

'Wow, you're a natural!'

Kevin was already getting the hang of it. When his mum brought the ball back into the room, he reached his hands up towards her. It was *his* ball now and he wanted another go!

KICK! He managed to lift the ball up into the air and it bounced off a table lamp.

'How on earth did you do that?' Anna asked in shock but Kevin just clapped and giggled.

'It's a good thing that ball is soft!' Herwig laughed.

The De Bruynes had a new footballer in the family. As Kevin got older, his interest only increased. Whenever there was a match on TV, his eyes were glued to the action.

'Son, don't sit so close to the screen,' his dad told him but he didn't budge an inch.

'Kevin. . . *KEVIN!*'

When Kevin watched football, it was like he was

under a magic spell. He was so absorbed that he didn't notice what was going on around him.

'Sorry!' he apologised, snapping out of his daze. Even as he shifted his body back, he kept his eyes fixed on the screen.

Kevin loved watching football but he loved playing football even more. Once his kicks grew too powerful for the living room, his football games moved outside to the back garden. And as soon as he turned six, his parents took him along to train with their local club in north-west Belgium, KVV Drongen.

Kevin was really excited to test himself against the other boys in the neighbourhood. He already knew that football was his game, but was he good at it? And if so, how good? There was only one way to find out.

First up – passing. Kevin cushioned the ball nicely with the side of his right foot and then played an accurate pass back to his partner.

'Excellent work!' the coach praised him.

Next up – dribbling. Kevin weaved his way through the cones, keeping the ball under close control. Other boys slowed right down to avoid knocking them over, but not Kevin. He was flying! He had practised this drill in the garden with his dad.

'Excellent work!' the coach praised him.

Next up – shooting. As Kevin waited for his turn, he watched the boys ahead of him in the line. They were all taking an extra touch to control the coach's pass.

'No, I'm going to strike it first time,' Kevin decided.

He was feeling confident and he was desperate to stand out. *Bang! GOAL!*

'Excellent work!' the coach praised him.

At last, it was time for the big finale – the match. Kevin was the new kid in the team but as soon as the game kicked off, his competitive edge kicked in.

'I'm in space – pass!' he called out again and again until he got the ball.

'Make a run!' he told his attackers.

'Don't just hoof it!' he told his defenders.

Kevin was trying to get the best out of his teammates. At first, they didn't like it one bit.

'Who does this new kid think he is, telling us what to do all the time?' they thought.

However, they didn't say that out loud because thanks to Kevin, they were winning. He ran and ran from box to box, his sweaty blond hair bobbing up and down. He set up goals and he scored goals too.

'Excellent work!' the coach praised him.

Kevin's amazing football skills made him lots of new friends. Suddenly, it wasn't just him and his parents having a kickaround in the garden; it was him and all the other KVV Drongen Under-7s!

'Please be careful near my flowerbeds,' the neighbour asked politely, but the boys didn't listen.

'Kevin. . . Oh, for goodness sake – *KEVIN!*'

He was under one of his football magic spells again. He was so absorbed that he didn't notice what was going on around him.

'Sorry!' he apologised, snapping out of his daze. It was too late, though; the damage had already been done. The flowerbeds were ruined.

As a punishment, the boys had to switch from a leather ball to a plastic one. It was much gentler on the plants but a lot less fun for the footballers. If it was windy, the plastic ball would float off or swerve strangely through the air. When they kicked it, it was impossible to predict what would happen next.

In the end, Kevin and his neighbour came up with a brilliant compromise.

'You can go back to playing with a leather ball,' said the neighbour, 'but only if you all kick with your weaker feet.'

'Deal!'

For Kevin, that was his left foot. At first, it felt weird not using his right foot but he soon got used to it. Before long, he had two fantastic feet to choose from. Kevin was already preparing himself for his career as a professional footballer.

CHAPTER 3

GOING TO GENT

Several times on the journey to Drongen, Jan Van Troos thought about turning his car round. The rain was falling heavily and it had been for days now. The windscreen wipers were working as fast as they could but they were fighting a losing battle against the downpour.

'This better be worth it,' Van Troos muttered through gritted teeth.

If it was bad weather for driving, then it was terrible weather for a children's football match. At best, the pitch would be a mud bath; at worst, it would be one giant puddle.

It was only the fear of missing out that kept the

Gent scout going. What if this kid was 'the next big thing' and he ended up signing for a rival club instead? No, he couldn't let that happen, even on a miserable day like this.

When he arrived, Van Troos stayed in his car for as long as possible. It was only when the match was about to kick off when he put his umbrella up, and make a mad dash for the touchline.

Van Troos didn't even know the name of the KVV Drongen player that he was there to watch, but he preferred it that way.

'I'll know him when I see him play,' he liked to say.

Instead of one giant puddle, the pitch turned out to be a series of smaller puddles with squelchy mud islands in between. Most of the boys stood shivering in their soaked-through shirts, waiting for the match to be over. A blond boy in the Drongen midfield, however, was getting on with the game. He was in the zone, splashing his way forward like he hadn't even noticed the rain.

'That's the one I'm here to watch,' Van Troos decided very quickly.

Not only did the kid clearly love playing football, but he was also very, very good at it. He was one of the smallest players on the pitch and yet he was bravely winning tackles and chipping passes out of the puddles. Some were short and snappy, and some were long and powerful. Some were with his right foot and some were with his left foot. All of them, however, were clever and accurate passes.

'That playmaker's got vision!' the scout exclaimed.

Sadly, not all of his teammates shared his talent, or his passion.

'Come on, keep going!' the boy shouted, trying to lift their spirits and spread his will to win.

Van Troos was so impressed that he too started to forget about the rain. Scouting was all worth it for moments like this. He had found Belgium's 'next big thing'!

The best footballers weren't necessarily the ones with lots of tricks and flicks; they were the ones who made the beautiful game look simple.

At the final whistle, Drongen were the winners, all thanks to their blonde midfield dynamo. After a quick word with the team's coach, Van Troos introduced himself to Kevin's dad.

'Wow, what a performance, especially in these conditions! Your son has a very bright future ahead of him. Do you think he would be interested in coming along to train with us at Gent?'

'The Buffalos' were one of the biggest teams in Belgium. The senior side played in the First Division. Herwig knew what Kevin's answer would be but he still pretended to think about the question.

'Yes, I think he'd like that,' he replied calmly.

When his dad told him the great news, Kevin's reply wasn't calm at all.

'Yes, Yes, YES!' he whooped out of the car window. 'I'm going to play for Gent! I'm going to play for Gent!'

Kevin would be sad to say goodbye to his friends, but he was ready for a new football challenge. He wasn't worried about playing at a higher level; he was excited. Going to Gent would mean better teammates, better opponents, better training sessions, and hopefully, better pitches to play on.

CHAPTER 4

LIVERPOOL DREAMS

Kevin soon settled into his new life at Gent. At the age of eleven, he led his team all the way to the Belgian Youth Cup final. The big game would be played at a professional football stadium, Le Canonnier in Mouscron.

'Whoa, this place is huge!' Kevin's teammate, Simon, marvelled as they took a tour around the ground. 'How many people can you fit in here – 50,000?'

'No, it only holds 10,000,' Kevin corrected him. He had done his homework. 'I really don't think our match is going to be a sell-out, though!'

'Hey, you never know!' Simon replied optimistically.

The Gent youngsters got changed into their blue-and-white kits in Royal Mouscron's massive home dressing room and then made their way out onto the pitch for the warm-up. As he walked out of the tunnel, Kevin imagined the roar of a waiting crowd. 'One day!' The playing surface was soft but not so soft that their studs sank in. The immaculate green grass seemed to go on and on forever.

'I could get used to playing on a pitch like this!' Kevin thought to himself, remembering the old days at Drongen.

As he jogged and stretched, a TV camera followed his every move. How did they know that Kevin was Gent's star player?

'Hey kid, are you happy to answer a few questions?' the cameraman called out.

'Sure,' Kevin said with a shrug. If he was going to be a professional footballer when he was older, he would need to get used to giving interviews.

'Great! So, what club would you like to play for when you're older?'

Wearing a baggy Umbro jumper, Kevin spoke

clearly and confidently into the microphone. 'My favourite club is Liverpool and my favourite player is Michael Owen. I would love to play there one day!'

Kevin didn't just like Liverpool; he *loved* Liverpool. It was the club that his mum and granddad had supported when they lived in England, and they had passed their passion on to him. For each birthday and Christmas, Kevin was allowed to pick one present from the club catalogue. Soon, his bedroom was like a mini-Anfield.

He had Liverpool curtains, Liverpool bedcovers, Liverpool posters on the walls. And in his wardrobe, Kevin kept his prized collection of Liverpool shirts. His favourite was the one with '10 OWEN' on the back. How cool would it be to follow in his hero's footsteps?

'One step at a time,' Kevin told himself.

First, he had a final to win for Gent. They were up against Genk, a club from the north-east of Belgium. With the TV cameras rolling, Kevin was determined to put on a match-winning performance. He ran and ran, looking for the space to do something really special.

When a Gent defender booted a long ball forward, the Genk goalkeeper rushed out to reach it first. He was outside his penalty area, however, so he couldn't pick it up. Instead, he chested the ball as far away as possible.

It landed right in front of Kevin. He was near the halfway line but he didn't doubt himself for a second. He had plenty of power in his little legs. *Bang!* Kevin kicked the ball past the goalkeeper and past the last defenders, and it rolled into the back of the net.

Goooooooooooooooooooaaaaaaaaaaaaaaaaalllllllllllll llllllllllllll!!!!!!!!!!!!!!!!!!!

That was really special! Kevin punched the air and then raised his arms above his head like a champion. The other Gent players raced over to celebrate with their star Number 7

'What a strike!' Simon cheered, hugging the hero.

Kevin was off the mark but that was just the start of his man-of-the-match display. In the second half, he dribbled forward, danced through a tackle, and angled his shot into the far corner.

*Gooooooooooooooooooooaaaaaaaaaaaaaaaaalllllllllllll
lllllllllllllll!!!!!!!!!!!!!!!!!!!!!!*

Gent won the final 6–2, with Kevin scoring
four times. At the final whistle, he jumped for joy.
They were the young Champions of Belgium! The
team sprinted over and slid on their knees in front
of their families. Once the trophy was theirs, they
carried it together on a full lap of honour around Le
Canonnier.

Campiones, Campiones, Olé! Olé! Olé!

After that, it was time for Kevin's second interview
of the day. His hair was a little sweatier and his face
was a little redder, but he sounded just as clear and
confident as before.

'Genk are a very good team and it was a difficult
match,' he explained, just like an experienced star.
'We took our chances and scored good goals.'

In the team photo at the end, Kevin stood at the
back next to his coach, proudly wearing his winners'
medal around his neck. Like the TV interviews,
that was something that he'd soon get used to as a
professional footballer.

CHAPTER 5

STUBBORN STAR

Even at that early age, Kevin already had his life plan sorted. 'I want to stay at this school until I'm fourteen,' he told his mum, 'and then I want to go to a sports school until I'm eighteen. After that, I'll be a full-time footballer!'

When he put it like that, it sounded so simple. However, becoming a top professional player was anything but simple. It was a one-in-a-million chance but Kevin was so determined to succeed. He would do whatever it took to become the world's best playmaker, 'the next Zinedine Zidane'.

Zidane, the French midfield maestro, was Kevin's new number one hero, after his match-winning performance for Real Madrid in the 2002 Champions League final against Bayer Leverkusen. Zidane glided around the pitch, controlling the game with his brilliant passes. He was always one step ahead of his opponents, finding gaps that no-one else had even spotted.

'Like me!' Kevin thought to himself as he watched the game at home in Drongen.

When he got the ball, 'Zizou' seemed to have all the time in the world. No-one could get it off him.

'Like me!' Kevin thought to himself. He had forgotten all about the game going on, and the other twenty-one players on the pitch. His eyes were fully focused on Zidane, following his every touch and move.

And when his team needed a hero, Zidane rose to the challenge.

'Like me!' Kevin thought to himself.

Zidane's winning goal was the best goal that Kevin had ever seen. As Roberto Carlos crossed from the left, the Frenchman waited calmly on the edge of the penalty area. As the ball fell from the sky, Zidane

watched it carefully onto his weaker left boot. *Bang!*
The technique was perfect and the volley flew into
the top corner.

Kevin's jaw dropped – he was absolutely speechless.
What a hero! He couldn't wait to go outside and
practise that volley. He had work to do.

'That's going to be me one day!' Kevin promised
himself.

Before he achieved that dream, however, he had
some crucial lessons to learn about losing and listening.

For Kevin, winning was the most important thing
in the world. It was what football was all about. In
every match he played, he worked and worked to get
the result that he wanted. Nothing would stop him,
except the final whistle.

Thanks to Kevin, Gent did win a lot of matches
but they couldn't win every single match. That was
impossible! As the new Champions of Belgium, 'The
Buffalos' travelled to the Netherlands for a special
football tournament.

'These games are going to be tough,' Frank De
Leyn, the youth coach, warned his young players

before kick-off. 'It's all good experience and the most important thing is that you enjoy yourselves today!'

Kevin couldn't wait to test himself against the top teams from other countries. This was the next step towards becoming 'The Next Zidane' and he was ready for it. Unfortunately, some of his teammates were not. With Gent losing, Kevin grew angrier and angrier.

'No, pass to *me!*' he screamed at his teammates.

'What are you doing? Tackle him!'

When the match finished, Kevin sat down in the middle of the pitch and refused to move. He was furious with his friends. The defeat was the whole team's fault.

'Come on, the next match is about to start!' De Leyn called out but Kevin refused to budge. In the end, Herwig had to run on and take his son off the field.

'That is not the right way to behave,' his dad said sternly, sounding very disappointed. 'I know you love to win but you have to learn to lose too. It's part of life and it happens to everyone, including Zidane.'

'But my team let me down!' Kevin complained.

'No son, *you* let your team down,' Herwig
corrected him.

Once he had calmed himself down, Kevin saw
that his dad was right. No-one liked a bad loser. He
had to be gracious in defeat, no matter how painful
that felt. Football was only a game, after all. And if
he really wanted to make his team better, he had to
help his teammates, not criticise them constantly.

'I'm sorry, guys,' he said, looking shamefully down
at his feet.

'We forgive you,' his teammates replied. Without
their stubborn star, they were losing again. 'Now, get
out there and help us win!'

Kevin learnt his second crucial lesson on another
trip abroad. That time, the Gent youth team were at
a training camp in Spain. After a long, hot practice,
he was looking forward to chilling out in the shade
with an ice-cold drink.

'Can you help collect the balls and cones, please?'
De Leyn asked politely at first.

'No, I'm hot,' he replied rudely.

'Kevin, I'm asking you to do something for the team – help collect the balls and cones, please.'

'Why can't someone else do it?' he moaned.

'Because it's your turn, and it will only take you two minutes. Just do it!'

On Kevin's list of least favourite things, it went:

1. Losing

2. Being told what to do.

He was Gent's star player, so why should he do something that he didn't want to do? He turned and walked away.

'Kevin! *KEVIN!*'

De Leyn was livid. How dare a young player disobey his coach like that? Kevin wasn't going to get away with such disrespect.

'You might think you're undroppable,' De Leyn told him, 'but you're not. If you don't listen to me and do what I say, I'll send you home right now!'

This was so unfair! Kevin stormed over to the goalposts in protest. He held on tightly and refused to let go. In the end, it took three Gent coaches to pull him away.

De Leyn sat his stubborn star down for a telling-off.

'That is not the right way to behave,' he said sternly, sounding very disappointed. 'No player is bigger than the team, not even Zidane. He didn't win the World Cup on his own, or the Champions League. Football is all about working together to win. That strong will of yours will carry you all the way to the top, but only if you use it correctly. When people are trying to help you, listen!'

Once he had calmed himself down, Kevin saw that his coach was right. No-one liked a stroppy, selfish player. If he really wanted to become the best playmaker in the world, he had to work hard for the team, even if that meant collecting the balls and cones.

'I'm sorry,' Kevin said, looking shamefully down at his feet.

'I forgive you,' De Leyn replied. 'Now, get out there and help us win!'

CHAPTER 6

GENT TO GENK

When it came to achieving his goals, Kevin wasn't afraid to travel. That independent spirit was something that his mum had passed on to him, just like her love of Liverpool. Anna was born in Burundi, Africa, and grew up in the Ivory Coast and then England. She had only moved to Belgium as an adult when she met Herwig.

'Always chase your dreams!' she told her son.

When Kevin was out on the pitch looking for a pass, he picked the best option, rather than the easiest one. He treated his football career in exactly the same way. The easiest option was to stay at Gent and work his way up through the youth teams to the

Under-21s, and then from the Under-21s to the first team. The path was set out in front of him and all he had to do was follow it.

That's not what Kevin did, however. Instead, he left Gent behind. It was 2005, and after six years at the club, he'd had enough. The coaches were always criticising him for something –

dribbling too much,

passing too much,

shouting too much,

working too hard,

not working hard enough...

He couldn't win! Why couldn't they just let him be? He knew that the coaches were only trying to help him improve, but Kevin just wanted to be Kevin. He had learnt to lose and he had learnt to listen, but at times, he was still a stubborn star.

'I like Genk's style,' Kevin told his parents. 'I want to go and play for them.'

Although Gent had won that youth cup final, Genk played better, passing football. With Kevin as their new playmaker, they would be unstoppable.

The Racing Genk senior team had just finished third in the Belgian First Division, and they would be playing in the UEFA Cup the following season. Not only that, but 'The Smurfs' had got there with a young, inexperienced squad. Star striker Kevin Vandenbergh was twenty-one, Faris Haroun was twenty and Steven Defour was only sixteen!

So, for an ambitious fourteen-year-old like Kevin, moving to Genk made total sense. He believed that his road to the first team would be quicker there. His goal was to follow in Steven's footsteps, and when it came to achieving his goals, Kevin wasn't afraid to travel.

Gent to Genk – the two names were so similar but in terms of distance, the two cities were 100 miles apart. To get to training and back, that would be 200 miles every day – impossible! No, Kevin would have to leave his family home in Drongen behind.

'Behave yourself,' his dad said as they dropped him off at his new club lodgings in Genk. 'We'll come and watch all your games at the weekends.'

'I'm proud of you,' his mum told him, kissing him

on the cheek. 'Keep chasing your dream!'

Going from Gent to Genk, Kevin landed in football heaven. He was sharing a house with other members of the youth team, and when they weren't at training, they were out playing together in the local park. If they got too tired to play real football, they just played FIFA on the Playstation instead. Plus, there were no parents telling them to stop and do their homework!

One of his housemates was Steven Defour, the sixteen-year-old who was already playing for the Genk first team. Kevin wanted to know everything about his experience.

'How hard are the training sessions?'

'What did the manager say to you?'

'What are the senior players like?'

Steven was surprised by all the questions, but also impressed. Most of the other youngsters were too shy to say more than a few words to him, but this kid was sure of himself. He knew that he was going to be a professional footballer, and he was willing to put in the hard work to get there.

As soon as he saw him play, Steven understood where Kevin's confidence came from. The kid was so talented that it took him a while to work out which was his weaker foot. He seemed to prefer his right but his left was just as powerful and accurate.

'Wow, that kid's special!' Steven thought to himself. Soon, other people at Genk were thinking the same thing.

CHAPTER 7

PROJECT 2000

At the turn of the twenty-first century, Belgian
football was in a bad state. At the 1998 World Cup,
the national team had drawn all three of their group
matches against the Netherlands, Mexico and South
Korea, and went home early. Then at Euro 2000,
Belgium were the tournament hosts but even the
support of the home crowd couldn't save them;
'The Red Devils' lost to Italy and Turkey, and were
knocked out in the first round again.

'Something has to change!' former Belgian
international Michel Sablon told Michel D'Hooghe,
the president of the Belgian FA.

Hard work and experience was getting them

nowhere. The team captain, Lorenzo Staelens, was thirty-six. The goalkeeper was thirty-five, midfielder Marc Wilmots was thirty-one, and striker Luc Nilis was thirty-three. Soon, all four would retire, and what then? Belgium needed more skill, more magic. The Mpenza brothers, Émile and Mbo, were promising young attackers, but they couldn't lead the country to glory on their own. Where had all the talent gone?

'I agree, but what do we change, and how do we change it?' D'Hooghe asked.

Together, Sablon and youth coach Bob Browaeys came up with 'Project 2000', a bold plan to develop a talented new generation of Belgian footballers. To achieve that ambitious aim, they introduced two key changes.

The first key change was style. In 1998 and 2000, Belgium had played a boring 4-4-2 formation, sometimes even a 5-3-2 against the top teams. They sat back and defended deep, hoping to score a header from a free kick or a corner. The nation hated watching such dull football. It was so old-fashioned.

The people wanted modern entertainment.

'From now on, we play to win,' Sablon argued, 'rather than holding on for a draw!'

'Project 2000' changed the whole of Belgian football, from the senior national squad all the way down to the local youth clubs. Suddenly, every team switched its formation from 4-4-2 to 4-3-3, and its focus from defence to attack. It was a football revolution!

To play better attacking football, however, Belgium would need better attacking footballers. Browaeys and his fellow youth coaches did everything they could to help kids to develop their skills and play with freedom. Instead of big 11 vs 11 matches, they played smaller games: 8 vs 8, 5 vs 5, even 2 vs 2!

With less space and lots more touches, it was all about technique and creativity.

Daring dribbles, difficult diagonal balls – 'Go for it!' the coaches encouraged.

One-twos, possession passing – 'Go for it!' the coaches told them.

Kevin loved every second of that freedom. Yes, he was still a stubborn star at times, but he was exactly the kind of footballer that Sablon and Browaeys were looking for – a born winner with exceptional talent.

'Watch how he reads the game,' Browaeys admired from the sideline. 'He's only fifteen and he's already three steps ahead of everyone else. Look at that pass, that vision!'

Kevin became one of Project 2000's top talents, alongside a skilful winger called Eden Hazard. Together, they were the bright future of Belgian football. With players like Kevin and Eden, the national team would be able to entertain the people *and* win.

'How exciting is that?' Sablon asked enthusiastically.

Very! The Belgian people didn't mind missing out on Euro 2004 and World Cup 2006 if it meant that they would have a chance of winning Euro 2016 and World Cup 2018. The Red Devils were building for the future.

Project 2000's second key change was education.

In Genk, Kevin was lucky enough to go to one of the new Topsport schools, with Steven and other members of the youth team, including goalkeeper Thibaut Courtois.

Sint-Jan Berchmans College offered the best of both worlds – studies *and* sport. Kevin still had to do all of the normal classes, but he also got to play a lot more football. There were extra training sessions every day with the Racing Genk coaches, where he worked on improving every aspect of his game.

'It's amazing here – I'm learning so much!' Kevin told his mum on the phone.

'That's wonderful news,' Anna replied. 'I'm expecting great results in your Maths exams now!'

'Oh sorry, I was talking about the football!' her son said.

As a poster boy for Project 2000, Kevin was on a fast track to the top.

CHAPTER 8

NOT MESSING AROUND

When Kevin left Gent, his old youth coach sent a warning message to his new youth coach at Genk, Roland Breugelmans:

'He's a very good player but he's not always easy to work with.'

Breugelmans already knew what to expect from Kevin. He had seen him in action many times over the years. Yes, Kevin could be very stubborn at times but with the right kind of coaching, Breugelmans was sure that the boy's special talent would shine through.

The Genk Academy was the perfect place for him. The players weren't allowed to wear the latest

colourful, flashy footwear; it was black boots only.
In order to become a star, you had to prove it on the
pitch, and in training too.

'Get a move on!' Breugelmans yelled. 'We haven't
got all day!'

Kevin moaned and dragged his feet around the
edge of the field. On his list of least favourite things,
it went:

1. Losing
2. Being told what to do
3. Fitness work in training.

In a competitive match, he always ran from the first
minute to the last. But when there was no football
in sight, what was the point? It felt like a waste of
precious energy, and so did the sprint ladders, and the
weight-lifting, and the squats, and the...

'You'll thank me when you get to the first team,'
Breugelmans told his stubborn star. 'If you don't
build up your strength, the defenders will eat you
alive!'

At youth level, however, the defenders couldn't
get close to Kevin. When he got the ball in midfield,

he glided forward gracefully like Zidane. Would he pass with his left foot or his right? His opponents never knew because Kevin had two magic wands. *Abracadabra!* With one tap of a side-foot, he slipped the ball into a gap that no-one else had spotted, for a teammate that no-one else had spotted.

'Wow, that kid's special!' Breugelmans thought to himself.

Not everyone at Genk shared his opinion, however. Every April, the coaches met up to discuss the progress of their young players. For the first few years, Kevin was the subject of a heated debate.

'He thinks he knows everything. His attitude sucks!' one side would argue.

'Yes, he can be difficult at times but you can't question his commitment, or his talent!' the other side would reply.

Luckily, Kevin's supporters always outnumbered his haters. And the older he got, the better he became. Once he reached the Genk Under-21s, there was no stopping him, or his partner in attack, Christian Benteke.

They were a perfect match. Kevin was the pass-master, the playmaker, the King of the Assists; and Christian was the big, powerful target man. Together, they scored goal after goal after goal.

Kevin's cross from the left landed right on Christian's head. *GOAL!*

Christian chested the ball down for Kevin to strike. *GOAL!*

Kevin split the defence with a perfect pass through to Christian. *GOAL!*

With every match-winning double act, they were getting closer and closer to the Genk first team.

'I'll be playing with you soon!' Kevin told Steven confidently, and his friend didn't doubt it.

When Kevin got his first invitation to train with the seniors, he wasn't nervous at all. He had been expecting the call-up for a while, and he had earned it. Ultimately, it was just another chance to play football, and football was his game.

Kevin didn't say much as he got changed in the dressing room. That didn't surprise the Genk players. They had seen lots of youngsters freeze when they first came face-to-face with the first-team stars. It was a scary, make-or-break moment.

'They've got no idea!' Steven smiled to himself. He wasn't going to spoil the fun.

Off the pitch, Kevin was super chilled. He rarely spoke unless he had something to say. On the pitch, however, he was a completely different character.

'Yes, over here, pass it to me!' Kevin called out to his new teammates straight away.

That *did* surprise the Genk players. This kid wasn't as quiet and shy as they had thought! However, it was only a casual five-a-side practice match, so they let him get away with it.

Kevin didn't stop there, though. This was football and he wasn't messing around. As he dribbled forward with the ball, he looked around for options. Why weren't his teammates making runs? Well, if they were too lazy to move themselves, he would have to help them.

'Get into space!' Kevin yelled, pointing at gaps in the defence.

This time, the Genk players weren't just surprised;

they were *stunned*. This seventeen-year-old had a lot of nerve to order his seniors around like that. Where was the respect?

'Who does this new kid think he is, telling us what to do all the time?' they muttered moodily.

'Come on, MOVE!' Kevin moaned. He wanted to win and he didn't care who he had to shout at to make that happen.

Once his new teammates recovered from the shock, they really enjoyed playing with Kevin. He made football look so simple and fun. He always seemed to have his next incredible pass planned in his head – to the left, to the right, or straight through the middle of the defence. All he needed was willing runners. *GOAL!*

'Fair enough, that kid's pretty special!' the Genk players thought to themselves.

Kevin had won them over with a midfield masterclass. Yes, he was a bit bold and brash, but he was also brilliant.

CHAPTER 9

COMING SOON

As the 2008–09 season came to an end, Genk sat in eighth place in the Belgian First Division. 'The Smurfs' were safe from relegation but too far behind the Top Four European places. With two games still to go, the manager Pierre Denier decided to change things up. It didn't matter if Genk won or lost, so why not try something new?

'It's the perfect chance to give our kids some game-time,' he told the youth coaches. 'How about De Bruyne – do you think he's ready?'

Breugelmans laughed. 'He certainly thinks he is!'

Kevin was training with the first team, so why wasn't he playing matches for them too? That was the question that he kept asking the youth coaches. As soon as he achieved one target, he moved straight on to the next. Now that he was so close to his senior debut, Kevin was more determined than ever. So what if he was only seventeen? Michael Owen was seventeen when he made his debut for Liverpool and he'd scored. If he was good enough, he was old enough.

Denier shrugged, 'Sure, why not? Let's see what he's made of!'

When he heard the news, Kevin jumped for joy. This was it – the opportunity that he'd been waiting impatiently for!

'Mum, Dad, I'm about to become a professional footballer!' he shouted down the phone.

Once he met up with the squad, however, Kevin was back to his normal, super-chilled self.

It was no big deal, travelling on the team coach with all the experienced internationals.

It was no big deal, seeing his blue-and-white shirt hanging in the dressing room – '7 DE BRUYNE'.

It was no big deal, going out to warm up on the

pitch in front of the fans.

It was no big deal, seeing his name there on the list of Genk substitutes.

As the game kicked off, Kevin watched and waited. He soon had a new entry on his list of least favourite things:

1. Losing
2. Being told what to do
3. Sitting on the bench.

It was *so* boring! Kevin wasn't used to it. For the youth teams and the Under-21s, he always played every minute because he was the main man, the star playmaker. Now all he could do was cross his fingers and hope for the best.

It was still 0–0 at half-time but early in the second-half, Genk went 2–0 down. Kevin kept looking over at Denier – what was his manager thinking? What changes would he make, and when?

After sixty minutes, Goran Ljubojević came on for Jelle Vossen.

After seventy minutes, Dániel Tőzsér came on for Hans Cornelis.

And finally, after eighty minutes, Kevin came on for Ederson.

As he ran onto the field, he felt a big burst of pride, passion and adrenaline. Was there still time to turn the game around?

It certainly wasn't the dream debut that Kevin had been hoping for. There were only 7,000 fans in the stadium and the pitch wasn't much better than that Drongen pitch where Jan Van Troos had first scouted him. Plus, his team was losing. Two minutes after he came on, Charleroi attacked and scored again. 3–0!

'Come on, we're making this way too easy for them!' Kevin moaned.

Yes, it was only his first game but he always wanted to win. He didn't care who he had to shout at to make that happen. Sadly, it was too little too late. The referee blew the final whistle before Kevin could really show off his killer passing.

'I wasn't even out there long enough to sweat!' he thought to himself as he shook hands with his opponents.

Kevin was disappointed with a defeat on his debut,

but he focused on the positives. He was a Genk first-team player now – he had a shirt number to prove it.

'Well played,' Denier said, patting him on the back.

When would Kevin's next chance arrive? For the last game of the season, he was back on the bench. This time, Genk were playing at home at the Cristal Arena. Was a dream home debut on the cards? There was definitely a better atmosphere in the stadium. Some 23,000 fans were there to cheer on The Smurfs against the top team in Belgium, RSC Anderlecht.

Genk were 1–0 down at half-time and 2–0 down after sixty minutes. Kevin's legs were getting restless. He kept looking over at Denier – what was his manager thinking? What changes would he make, and when?

After sixty-one minutes, Ivan Bošnjak came on for Hans Cornelis.

After seventy-two minutes, Adam Nemec came on for Goran Ljubojević.

And finally, after eighty-three minutes, Kevin came on for Stein Huysegems.

Was there still time for him to turn the game around? No, the match finished 2–0, and it was two defeats out of two for Kevin. Although he hated losing, he knew that neither result had been his fault. In both games, Genk were already 2–0 down when he came on. What was he supposed to do in ten minutes? His feet were magical but they weren't *that* magical.

In order to get the best out of Kevin, they needed to play him from the start. Only then would he be able to control the game and show off his full passing range.

'Well done, you're almost there!' Breugelmans congratulated him. The youth coach had always believed in his stubborn star.

Kevin's time was coming soon. He couldn't wait for the 2009–10 season to start.

CHAPTER 10

THE BIG BREAKTHROUGH

It didn't take long for the new Genk manager Hein Vanhaezebrouck to notice Kevin's incredible potential. By now, it was impossible to miss. In their pre-season practice matches, the eighteen-year-old stole the show.

'Wow, that kid's special!' Vanhaezebrouck thought to himself.

With the ball at his feet, Kevin could do anything and everything: he could control the game with short, sharp passes; he could change the game with long, perfect passes; he could dribble through defences, and he could even shoot with either foot.

What made him truly special, however, was his vision. Kevin read the game so well that he always knew which of his many talents to use next.

'If he keeps improving,' the Genk manager told his coaches excitedly, 'he could be one of the best players in the world one day. He could even be the Johan Cruyff of his generation!'

Although Kevin preferred Zidane as a comparison, that was still amazing praise. In order to keep improving, however, he needed lots of game-time. Vanhaezebrouck gave him his first senior start in the first game of the 2009–10 season, but after that, he was back on the bench.

'Noooooooooo!' Kevin groaned.

It was frustrating to only play ten or fifteen minutes at the end, but Kevin needed to show his star quality at the top level. He needed to score a goal, or at least set one up with a killer pass. Only then would he get his big breakthrough.

Unfortunately, by the time that big breakthrough came, Vanhaezebrouck was gone. Fortunately, Genk's new manager, Franky Vercauteren, was a big fan of Kevin too. He gave his young star support and game-time.

At home against Standard Liège, Kevin's first shot of the game raced through the air like a rocket but it cannoned back off the crossbar.

'Oooooooooohhhh!' the Genk fans gasped, putting their hands to their heads.

In that moment, some players would have cursed their bad luck and lost their confidence. For Kevin, however, confidence was never a problem. That miss only spurred him on. He was getting closer and closer to that first goal.

A few minutes later, the ball dropped down in front of him, just outside the penalty area. Kevin didn't even think about a pass; he just pulled back his right foot and fired a shot goalwards. The fans in the Cristal Arena held their breath, but only for a split second, before they let out a massive cheer.

Goooooooooooooooooooaaaaaaaaaaaaaaaallllllllllll lllllllllllll!!!!!!!!!!!!!!!!!!!!

Top corner – what a strike! After watching the ball cross the line, Kevin turned away with his right arm in the air and his index finger pointing up at the sky. It was the calm celebration of someone who had already scored hundreds of goals, and yet it was actually his first-ever goal as a senior Genk player.

'At least give us a smile, mate!' his captain João Carlos teased.

That wonderstrike turned out to be the matchwinner, and the start of Kevin's big breakthrough. Suddenly, he was playing every game and creating magic in midfield.

In the next match between Genk and Standard Liège, Kevin dribbled inside off the left wing and threaded a perfect pass through the defence to Elyaniv Barda. 1–0 again!

'You're a genius!' the striker shouted as the pass-master jumped into his arms.

Kevin was on fire, and so were Genk. The Smurfs had only finished eleventh in the regular season but in the play-offs, they won five games out of six.

'We're on a roll, guys!' Kevin cheered happily.

He was playing a huge part in his team's success.

Against Sporting Charleroi, Kevin curled a cross straight onto Éric Matoukou's head. 2–0!

Fifteen minutes later, Kevin dribbled up the left wing yet again. He was having his best-ever game for Genk and he was determined to end it with something special. That's what the fans wanted too.

'Shoot! Shoot!' they urged.

On the edge of the penalty area, Kevin cut inside onto his right foot. As the defender rushed across to block his shot, Kevin fooled him by cutting back onto his left. He didn't have a weaker foot, just two magic wands. *Abracadabra!* With one strike of the boot, he fired the ball into the bottom corner.

Goooooooooooooooooooaaaaaaaaaaaaaaaaallllllllllll llllllllllllll!!!!!!!!!!!!!!!!!!!

The Cristal Arena went wild. What a wondergoal! This time, Kevin had a big smile on his face as he raced over to the corner flag to celebrate. He was already living out his childhood dream at the age of eighteen, and he was only just getting started.

'That was incredible, kid!' his teammate Dániel Tőzsér cried out.

The excitement was growing in Genk. They were through to the play-off final against Sint-Truiden and if they won, they would be playing in the Europa League next season. What a wonderful prize!

'Come on, we can do this!' Kevin called out in the dressing room before kick-off.

He wasn't keeping quiet anymore. This was their chance to qualify for one of Europe's biggest club competitions. Kevin wasn't at his brilliant best, but Genk still won.

'Europa League, here we come!' the players and fans cheered together at the final whistle.

Kevin couldn't wait.

CHAPTER 11

FUTURE OF BELGIAN FOOTBALL

Belgium's bright new football future didn't arrive overnight. Project 2000 was going to take some time. The senior team didn't make it to World Cup 2006, or Euro 2008. The Red Devils finished fifth in their qualifying group, behind Poland, Portugal, Serbia *and* Finland. The fans were furious – their football team had fallen so far.

'Don't worry, success is coming soon!' Sablon kept telling everyone.

Yet even at youth level, Belgium were still struggling to find their best form. In 2007, they made it to the Under-17 World Cup in South Korea but lost their group games against Tunisia and the USA.

'We've still got a long way to go,' Christian admitted to Kevin when he returned to Genk after the tournament.

The Belgium Under-19s didn't qualify for the European Championships in 2008, which meant they didn't go to the Under-20 World Cup either. A year later, they missed out on the European Championships in 2009 too, despite Eden and Christian's best efforts.

In 2010, it was Kevin's turn to try. Belgium started well with two 4–0 wins over Andorra and Kazakhstan. Even a 4–2 defeat to Norway didn't dampen their spirits too much.

'Come on, we can do this!' Kevin urged his teammates.

As always, he was getting the best out of the players around him, with his shouting and, most importantly, his amazing passing.

In the second qualifying round, Belgium were up against Croatia, Scotland and Montenegro. It was going to be tough because only the top team would go through to the tournament in France. Despite winning two out of three, the Red Devils could only finish second. Another year, another disappointment.

Kevin, however, was moving onwards and upwards. After two good games for the Under-21s, he was called up to the senior squad for a friendly match against Finland in August 2010.

Belgium had just missed out on World Cup 2010, their fourth major tournament in a row. After losing to Armenia and Estonia, the national coach Georges Leekens decided that it was time to change things up. It was a friendly, so why not try something new?

Leekens boldly picked his team for the future, the bright future of Belgian football – Vincent Kompany and Jan Vertonghen in defence, Kevin and Axel Witsel in midfield, and Eden, Christian and Romelu Lukaku in attack.

'What a line-up!' Belgium's young stars cheered. They couldn't wait to play together for their country.

Unfortunately, it wasn't the dream international debut that Kevin had been waiting impatiently for.

In the twelfth minute, Vincent accidentally deflected the ball into his own net. *1-0 to Finland!*

What could Kevin do to help turn things around? He tried his best to create something magical but after forty-five frustrating minutes on the right wing, he was taken off at half-time.

'Yes, we've still got a long way to go,' he admitted to Christian.

After that first brief taste of senior international football, Kevin didn't represent his country again for over a year. By then, Belgium had missed out on yet another tournament – Euro 2012. It was becoming a habit.

'No more excuses,' Vincent told his teammates firmly. 'We've now got the talent to compete at the top level, so let's prove it!'

The big turning point came in another friendly, this time against their neighbours, The Netherlands. When Kevin came on after fifty-six minutes, Belgium were losing 2–1. This time, he played a key role to help turn things around.

Dries Mertens stole the ball and scored. 2–2!

'Great work!' Kevin cheered, giving his friend a high-five.

Two minutes later, Dries passed to Romelu in the penalty area. 3–2!

The home fans at the Stade Roi Baudouin in Brussels went wild. Belgium were finally playing the brilliant football that Sablon and Browaeys had always dreamed of. Project 2000 was alive and kicking.

It was Kevin's turn to get involved. When he got the ball on the right wing, he looked up for players to pass to. Romelu? Mousa Dembélé? Dries? Dries was calling for it all the way over on the other side of the pitch, but Kevin knew that either of his magical feet could find him with a perfect pass. He went with his right and sent a thirty-yard diagonal ball straight onto Dries's chest. Dries pulled it back to Jan, who scored. 4–2!

'Thanks, mate!' Jan shouted, hugging Dries.

'Don't thank me,' he laughed. 'Thank Kevin – did you see that pass? Unbelievable!'

CHAPTER 12

BELGIUM'S BEST

Genk had only ever won the Belgian First Division title twice – in 1999 and 2002. Usually, The Smurfs finished mid-table but their manager Franky Vercauteren had a very good feeling about the 2010–11 season. Genk had three strong strikers – Elyaniv, Jelle Vossen and Marvin Ogunjimi – and, behind them, a young superstar in the making.

'This is your team now,' the manager told Kevin. 'I'm giving you all the freedom you need to go out there and create!'

He loved the sound of that. Freedom – it was all Kevin had ever wanted on the football pitch. Finally, he had the chance to play football his way.

In the first half against his old club Gent, a clearance landed at Kevin's feet on the left wing. He took two quick touches to move the ball goalwards, and then *BANG!* His fierce shot rose higher and higher, over the diving goalkeeper, and into the roof of the net.

Goooooooooooooooooooaaaaaaaaaaaaaaaalllllllllll llllllllllllll!!!!!!!!!!!!!!!!!!!

In the second half, Kevin got the ball on the right wing and played an incredible, long diagonal pass all the way out to Dugary Ndabashinze on the left. Dugary crossed to Jelle – 3–0!

'Easy!' Jelle joked as the trio celebrated together.

A week later against Charleroi, it was the Kevin, Jelle and Elyaniv Show.

Five defenders swarmed around Kevin like flies, trying and failing to stop him. That left Jelle free in the middle and Kevin picked him out perfectly. His pass cut through the defence like a knife through butter. 1–0!

Kevin's curling free kick clipped the far post and went in. 2–0!

Kevin angled a dangerous cross towards Jelle and the goalkeeper tipped it into his own net. 3–0!

Elyaniv soon added two more goals, and the second half had only just started! Genk's attack was simply unstoppable. They thrashed Eupen and Lierse to make it five wins out of five.

'We're top of the table!' Kevin boasted proudly.

Genk were 1–0 up against Club Brugge too, until their stubborn star lost his cool. Kevin got his first yellow card for a silly shirt pull.

'Okay, calm it down now,' Dániel warned him.

But Kevin didn't listen. Five minutes later, he flew in for a 50-50 ball and lost. Foul! As the referee ran over, he was already reaching into his pocket. Kevin stood there with his hands on his head and a look of shock on his face. He knew what was coming – a second yellow card, and then a red!

'No, no, NO!' Kevin muttered, shaking his head as he trudged off the pitch.

Yes, it was a harsh sending-off, but why had he rushed in for such a risky tackle? There was no need, and now Kevin had let his team down. With ten men, Genk could only draw the match 2–2.

When the other players returned to the dressing room after the final whistle, Kevin sat there silently in the corner, staring down at the floor. He didn't know what to say to his teammates. They had every right to be really angry with him. If it had been the other way around, Kevin would have been furious!

'I'm sorry, guys,' he said guiltily. 'It won't happen again, I promise.'

'Hey, we all make mistakes,' Dániel replied, giving him a pat on the back. 'You've learnt your lesson – now let's move on and win the league!'

When he returned from his one-match ban, Kevin went back to doing what he did best – setting up goals for his teammates.

Halfway through the season, Genk were still holding onto top spot, two points ahead of Anderlecht. Five poor performances later, however, and The Smurfs were down in second, with Gent and Lokeren creeping up behind them.

'Come on, it's time to bounce back!' Vercauteren

told the dressing room, but he was looking at one player in particular.

After an amazing start to the season, Kevin had lost his form and confidence. Genk needed him back to his best, and quickly. Luckily, his best was only ever a goal or an assist away...

Both came along at once, in the same match against Kortrijk. First, Kevin scored and then he set up Marvin.

'That's more like it!' he said to himself.

Kevin, and Genk, were back on track. He set up Marvin's winner against Brugge and Jelle's opening goal against Anderlecht. Kevin's passes were so clever and so perfect – the right angle, the right speed, the right place, the right time.

'You're the best!' Jelle yelled, hugging Kevin.

Genk finished one point behind Anderlecht in the regular season but they had still had the Championship Play-offs to go.

'Come on, we can still win this!' Kevin told his teammates passionately.

In 2010, he had come alive during the play-offs; in

2011, he exploded onto the world scene. Kevin set up three goals against Lokeren, one against Standard Liège, one against Gent, and, most importantly of all, Jelle's winner against Anderlecht.

'This is *our* year!' they cheered together.

However, the Belgian First Division title race still went down to the very last match of the season, Genk vs Standard Liège. If Genk won or drew, the trophy would be theirs. If they lost, however, the trophy would go to Standard instead.

'This is it, our final battle,' Vercauteren told his players before kick-off. 'You've worked so hard to get this far – don't let it slip now!'

As the teams walked out onto the pitch, the Jupiler Pro League trophy sat there in front of them, glistening in the light. Kevin looked away when he passed it.

'We have to win it first!' he thought to himself.

That looked unlikely at half-time because Standard were 1–0 up. Kevin was fuming as he stormed into the Genk dressing room. It was time to speak his mind, and he was never shy about doing that.

'We need to give absolutely everything in this second-half,' he shouted, 'EVERYTHING! We can't lose this, lads – not now!'

Despite Kevin's team-talk, Genk couldn't score. The minutes ticked by and time was running out. Kevin curled a clever free kick over the wall and it dipped down towards the bottom corner... but the Standard goalkeeper tipped it round the post.

'Ooooohhhhh!' the fans gasped, putting their hands to their heads.

Kevin, however, had no time to think 'what if' – he had a corner to take and he wanted to take it quickly. Instead of whipping the ball into the box, Kevin played it short to Dániel and caught the Standard defence daydreaming. Kennedy Nwanganga headed Dániel's cross powerfully past the goalkeeper. 1–1!

'Yes, yes, YES!' Kevin screamed, throwing his arms up in delight.

Genk were now less than fifteen minutes away from their third league title. They were the slowest fifteen minutes of Kevin's football career but he didn't stop running until the referee finally blew the full-time whistle.

'YAAAAAAAAAAAAAAAAAAY!' the crowd roared at an ear-splitting volume.

Genk were the Champions of Belgium – what a feeling! All their hard work had paid off. Kevin and his teammates ran around hugging each other and getting the party started.

Campiones, Campiones, Olé! Olé! Olé!

It was a night that they would never forget. Thousands of Genk fans flooded onto the pitch to celebrate with their heroes – Dániel, Dugary, Jelle, Elyaniv, Marvin, Kennedy and, of course, Kevin.

What an incredible season it had been for him – five goals, sixteen assists and a league title. It was now official; Kevin was one of Belgium's best.

CHAPTER 13

CHASED BY CHELSEA

Franky Vercauteren was delighted with Kevin's development. The Genk manager had shown real faith in his young playmaker and look what he had achieved already! The big problem now was holding on to his top title-winning talent. Europe's biggest clubs were circling around Kevin like sharks.

Piet de Visser was one of the most famous football scouts in the world. At PSV Eindhoven, the Dutchman had discovered two of Brazil's greatest ever strikers, Romário and Ronaldo, and now worked for Chelsea, focusing on the Dutch and Belgian leagues.

Kevin was eighteen when the scout first saw him play. As soon as he saw him in action, de Visser knew that he was watching a very special player. The midfielder had it all – a super first touch, two fantastic feet, and best of all, the vision to play killer passes. Kevin was one of the best players that he had ever scouted.

'You have to sign this kid,' de Visser told Chelsea's chief scout enthusiastically, showing him a highlight video. 'He's a revelation!'

Chelsea's chief scout, however, wasn't so sure. 'De Bruyne is very good,' he argued, 'but there are plenty of young playmakers like him.'

De Visser shook his head. 'No, no, no! This kid is better. Trust me, he's got something extra!'

How could he convince the chief scout? De Visser hoped that Kevin would have a great game when Genk travelled to Stamford Bridge in the Champions League in October 2011 but unfortunately, Chelsea thrashed The Smurfs 5–0.

'He's usually a lot better than that, I promise,' de Visser assured the Chelsea scouts.

Back in the Belgian league, Kevin was looking better than ever. In the first minute against Club

Brugge, he got the ball on the left side of the penalty area and attacked at speed. He dribbled inside on his right foot and pretended to shoot, but as the full-back jumped up to block it, Kevin rolled the ball calmly over to his left.

'Olé!' the Genk fans cheered. They loved to watch him fooling defenders like that. Kevin struck his shot so sweetly that the goalkeeper had no chance of stopping it.

Goooooooooooooooooooaaaaaaaaaaaaaaaalllllllllllll llllllllllllllll!!!!!!!!!!!!!!!!!!!

What a start! He jogged away with his arms up above his head like a champion. He would never get tired of scoring awesome goals.

'Please don't leave!' Jelle begged. 'We need you!'

With twenty minutes to go, Genk needed Kevin more than ever. They were losing 4–3. Could he create some more match-winning magic? Dugary's cross flew past Kennedy and Jelle, but not Kevin at the back post. He controlled the ball, bamboozled the poor full-back again, and blasted it high into the top corner.

*Goooooooooooooooooooooaaaaaaaaaaaaaaaaallllllllllll
lllllllllllllll!!!!!!!!!!!!!!!!!!!!*

What a fantastic finish – 4–4! Kevin ran over
to celebrate with the fans but he wasn't done yet.
There was still plenty of time left for him to grab the
winning goal, and complete his first-ever professional
hat-trick.

When Fabien Camus won the ball in midfield,
he only had one thought on his mind – where's
Kevin? He looked up and saw that his teammate
was bursting forward on the left, totally unmarked,
screaming 'Pass!' Kevin took a touch and then
chipped the ball coolly over the diving goalkeeper.

*Goooooooooooooooooooooaaaaaaaaaaaaaaaaallllllllllll
lllllllllllllll!!!!!!!!!!!!!!!!!!!!*

5–4 to Genk! As Kevin slid on his knees by the
corner flag, the Brugge defenders collapsed in defeat.
Game over – he was simply unstoppable.

Watching that game, de Visser knew that Chelsea
needed to act fast. If they didn't, they might lose him
to a rival team because Kevin was far too good to
stay at Genk much longer. At the right club, he could

reach the next level, and go from being Belgium's best to one of the world's best.

'That club is Chelsea!' the Dutch scout declared. He was sure of it. Kevin would be the perfect long-term replacement for their midfield legend, Frank Lampard.

The Genk director, Dirk Degraen, had already told de Visser that there were lots of other clubs chasing Kevin. It was very easy to see why. With time running out, de Visser made a bold decision. It was now or never.

'If the Chelsea scouts won't listen to me,' he thought, 'then I'll just have to take it right to the top!'

De Vissen sent the highlights video straight to the big boss, Roman Abramovich. Luckily, the Chelsea owner liked what he saw. Kevin was exactly the kind of exciting young footballer that he wanted in his team.

'De Bruyne has to come!' he told his chief scout firmly.

It was an order, not a suggestion. If Abramovich wanted to sign a player, then the deal was done.

For £7 million, Chelsea got themselves an absolute bargain. Kevin was delighted too.

'To come to a team like Chelsea is a dream,' he told the club website, 'but now I have to work hard to achieve the level that's necessary. This is one of the biggest clubs in the world.'

Kevin couldn't wait to take the next step towards footballing greatness. He had really enjoyed his seven years at Genk, but it was now time to test himself at a higher level. He had no doubt that he would rise to the challenge at Chelsea.

CHAPTER 14

GOING TO GERMANY

Kevin would have to wait for his Chelsea challenge, however. The club already had plenty of attacking midfielders to choose from – Juan Mata, Oscar, Florent Malouda, Yossi Benayoun, plus Kevin's Belgium teammate, Eden Hazard.

'Your time will come,' the Chelsea manager, Roberto Di Matteo, promised him.

Until then, Kevin was 'one for the future'. It was a phrase that he had always hated, but especially now that he was twenty years old. He had played over 100 first-team games, and he had won a league title. He was ready *now!* But after finishing the 2011–12 season at Genk, Kevin was loaned out to German club Werder Bremen instead.

'Welcome!' their manager Thomas Schaaf said warmly. 'We've heard great things about you!'

Bremen's Sporting Director, Klaus Allofs, had been keeping an eye on Kevin for years. When Chelsea made an offer to sign their midfielder Marko Marin, Allofs knew exactly who he wanted in exchange.

'Even if we only get him for a few months, that kid is top quality!' he assured Schaaf.

When he first arrived in Germany, however, Kevin wasn't his usual confident self. He was still a bit bitter about going out on loan. He was meant to be playing in the Premier League, not the Bundesliga.

'Look son, it's only for one year,' his dad reminded him. 'Think of it as a great opportunity to show Chelsea what they're missing. Make the most of it!'

Kevin decided to do just that. There was no point feeling sorry for himself; that wouldn't help his chances at Chelsea. All he could do was pick himself up and get back to doing what he did best – setting up goals for his new teammates.

Once Kevin found his magical feet at Bremen, it was wonderful to watch.

As he dribbled down the left wing, Kevin threaded one of his perfect through-balls. This one was so perfect that Aaron Hunt was able to hit it first-time. GOAL!

'Thanks, Kev!' Aaron cheered.

He swung a corner-kick high towards the back post, where Nils Petersen was waiting for an easy header. GOAL!

'Thanks, Kev!' Nils cheered.

He curled a fierce free kick into the box for Sebastian Prödl to nod home. GOAL!

'Thanks, Kev!' Sebastian cheered.

Marko Arnautović passed inside to Kevin, and Kevin passed straight back, cutting through the defence with a classic one-two. GOAL!

'Thanks, Kev!' Marko cheered.

In the crucial moments, Kevin found an extra bit of energy and an extra bit of magic, just like he had at Gent. He hated losing, and he loved being the hero.

'Come on, MOVE!' he moaned at his teammates, right from day one. Kevin wanted to win and he didn't care who he had to shout at to make that happen.

Bremen were losing 1–0 at home to Nürnberg, with seconds to go. That would be a terrible result, leaving them just one place above the relegation zone. So, Kevin raced forward, fired a shot at goal and Nils deflected it in. 1–1!

Away at Borussia Mönchengladbach, he saved the day again with a clever late cross to Aleksandar Ignjovski. 1–1!

'De Bruyne, De Bruyne!' the Bremen fans chanted at the top of their voices.

They didn't want their star Number 6 to leave after a year; they wanted to keep him forever. Kevin's killer passes were keeping them in the Bundesliga. What would they do without him? He wasn't just creating lots of chances for others; he was also scoring great goals of his own.

In his first game against Stuttgart, Kevin spun away from his marker, played a great one-two with Nils and then blasted the ball into the bottom corner.

Goooooooooooooooooooaaaaaaaaaaaaaaaaalllllllllllll llllllllllllllll!!!!!!!!!!!!!!!!!!!!

In his second game against Stuttgart, he lifted the ball over the left-back's head and chased after it. The goalkeeper raced off his line but Kevin got there first and lifted the ball over his head too!

Goooooooooooooooooooaaaaaaaaaaaaaaaaalllllllllllll llllllllllllllll!!!!!!!!!!!!!!!!!!!!

After that stubborn start, Kevin was really enjoying his time at Bremen. The Bundesliga was a few steps up from the Belgian league and it was the perfect preparation for life in the Premier League. The higher level didn't faze Kevin at all. Nothing ever did. Even when Bayern Munich were beating Bremen 4–0, he still kept playing the game his way. He scored their only goal in a 6–1 thrashing.

'I just hope Chelsea have been watching me!' Kevin told his dad.

As the season drew to a close, he said a stylish goodbye to German football. In the thirty-seventh minute of his final game for Bremen, Kevin raced on to Zlatko Junuzović's long ball and cheekily lobbed the keeper.

Gooooooooooooooooooooaaaaaaaaaaaaaaaallllllllllll llllllllllllll!!!!!!!!!!!!!!!!!!!!!!

Kevin wasn't done yet. As it was his last appearance for Bremen, he pulled out all his best tricks and flicks to entertain the fans. It was a fun farewell but also a sad one. How were the team going to cope without their star Number 6? It would be impossible to replace such a top talent.

'Thanks for all your hard work,' Allofs said, shaking his hand. 'We're really going to miss you!'

Kevin would miss Bremen too but London was calling. It was time to fight for his place in the Premier League. He had gained more experience in Germany and he had proved his point. Ten goals, nine assists and the Bundesliga Young Player of the Year award – surely, that all showed that Kevin was ready for his Chelsea challenge?

CHAPTER 15

ROAD TO THE WORLD CUP 2014

By the time Kevin returned to Chelsea, he had become a regular starter for Belgium. When The Red Devils missed out on a place at Euro 2012, it was clear that something was wrong. It was now over ten years since Belgium had qualified for a major tournament and it was starting to get embarrassing!

When Marc Wilmots became the new national team manager, he set about building a dream team. Their aim was simple – to make it all the way to the 2014 World Cup in Brazil. Anything less than that would be seen as a total failure.

'This is our golden generation,' the fans argued. 'If they can't do it, then we're doomed!'

Qualification wouldn't be easy, though. In Group A, Belgium were up against Croatia, Serbia, Wales, Scotland and Macedonia.

'At least we don't have to face Germany or Spain this time!' Eden admitted with relief.

That was true, but they couldn't get ahead of themselves. At international level, every match was difficult. Anyone could beat anyone.

Kevin was on the bench for Belgium's first games against Wales and Croatia, but he fought his way into the starting eleven against Serbia. And once he got there, he made sure that he kept his place.

Despite playing away from home, Wilmots picked an exciting, attacking line-up with Kevin, Eden and Nacer Chadli playing in behind the target man, Christian. The all-star strikeforce took a little while to find their rhythm but once they did, it was game over for Serbia.

Kevin was determined to leave his mark on the match, with a goal or an assist, or hopefully both! If he didn't, he would soon be back on the subs' bench.

'No, I can't let that happen!' he told himself.

When Nacer laid the ball back to him on the right wing, Kevin knew exactly what to do next, and so did Christian. It was years since they had played together for the Genk Under-21s but they hadn't lost that understanding. As Kevin curled a dangerous cross towards the back post, Christian escaped from his marker and headed it goalwards. The cross was so good that he couldn't miss the target. 1–0!

'Thanks mate, it's just like old times!' Christian laughed, hugging his friend.

Kevin was playing so well that Wilmots took Eden off instead. It was a bold decision but Kevin thanked his manager by sprinting into the penalty area and sliding the ball past the Serbian goalkeeper. 2–0!

Gooooooooooooaaaaaaaaaalllllllllllllllllllllllll!!!!!!!!!!!!

It wasn't just any goal; it was his first-ever international goal. Kevin was off the mark, two years after his debut against Finland, and boy did it feel good! He slid across the grass on his knees, punching the air. The whole team celebrated together.

'Come on lads, let's keep winning!' Vincent, their captain, cheered.

Belgium beat Scotland 2–0, and Kevin set up another header for Christian.

Belgium beat Macedonia 2–0, and this time, Kevin scored. He shrugged off the left-back, dribbled into the box and fooled the keeper at his near post.

Goooooooooooooaaaaaaaaaalllllllllllllllllllllll!!!!!!!!!!!!

'If you keep this up, you're going to kick me out of the team!' Eden joked but really, he was pleased for his friend. They had always dreamed of winning the World Cup together to prove the power of 'Project 2000'.

Kevin just couldn't stop starring for his country. He scored a diving header against Serbia and in Scotland, he set up a goal for another of his old Genk teammates, Steven Defour.

'I always knew that you'd be a top player!' Steven told Kevin with a huge grin on his face.

With one more win against Croatia, Belgium achieved their simple aim – to make it all the way to the 2014 World Cup.

'Brazil, here we come!' Kevin cried out as he rushed off the bench to join his joyous teammates on the pitch. They had all worked so hard for this. After twelve years of hurt, Belgium would be back where they belonged in football's greatest competition.

Allez la Belgique! Allez la Belgique!

Thousands of fans had travelled to Croatia for this massive moment. Finally, they could wave their national flags and scarves with pride again. They did so for hours in the stadium in Zagreb, as the players and coaches jumped up and down below them. They even popped champagne and put on T-shirts saying, 'Belgian Red Devils in Brazil'. As fireworks filled the sky, everyone sang together.

Allez la Belgique! Allez la Belgique!

When Kevin got back out on the football pitch, how did he celebrate World Cup qualification? By scoring one more goal in the final game against Wales. With four goals and four assists, he had risen from super sub to become Belgium's starting star. He was one of the first names on Wilmots's teamsheet, and the World Cup was less than a year away.

Kevin had proven himself for his country; now, it was time to do the same for his club.

CHAPTER 16

NO CHANCE AT CHELSEA

Kevin was excited about returning to Chelsea. His season at Werder Bremen had been a huge success and he was feeling more confident than ever. If he could conquer the Bundesliga, why not the Premier League too?

And yet Kevin nearly didn't leave Germany. The Young Player of the Year had caught the eye of Jürgen Klopp, the manager of Borussia Dortmund. Their star playmaker, Mario Götze, had just moved to Bayern Munich, and they needed a replacement. Kevin would be the perfect fit for Dortmund's attacking style but the new Chelsea manager refused to sell him.

'You'll get your chance here,' José Mourinho promised at a meeting in London. 'I believe in you!'

That was exactly what Kevin wanted to hear. He was playing brilliantly with Eden for Belgium, so why not for Chelsea too? The two of them were ready to take on the world together!

At first, everything went well back at Stamford Bridge. In July 2013, Kevin scored his first Chelsea goal in pre-season against Malaysia, and his second against AC Milan. Eden dribbled down the left and spotted Kevin in space on the right. Kevin didn't even take a touch to control the pass; he fired the ball straight past Christian Abbiati.

Goooooooooooooooooooooaaaaaaaaaaaaaaaaalllllllllllll llllllllllllll!!!!!!!!!!!!!!!!!!!!

The Chelsea fans were full of excitement for their Belgian double act.

'With Hazard and De Bruyne in attack, we can win the Premier League again!' they believed.

Mourinho seemed to think so too. He picked Kevin for the first game of the 2013–14 season against Hull City. He would play on the right, with

Eden on the left, Oscar in the middle, and Fernando Torres up front. What an amazing attack!

'I've got a good feeling about this!' Kevin declared in the dressing room before kick-off.

It didn't take him long to become a star at Stamford Bridge. Eden dribbled in from the left and played the ball through to Kevin. He nutmegged the defender to set up Oscar to score. 1–0 – they made it look so easy!

'What a pass!' Oscar cried out, pointing and smiling at Kevin.

At the final whistle, Chelsea had won 2–0 and Kevin had won the Man of the Match award. What a start to life in the Premier League!

After that, however, it all went downhill for Kevin. He didn't leave the bench against Aston Villa and he struggled to make an impact against Manchester United; after sixty minutes, Mourinho brought on Fernando instead.

'I wasn't playing *that* badly!' Kevin moaned. He hated to miss out on a single second of the action.

'Don't worry, we've got a long season ahead of

us,' Eden consoled his friend. 'Just be patient!'

But Kevin had never been a patient person, particularly not when it came to football. He wanted to play every minute of every match. Did Mourinho still believe in him? Kevin had his doubts, especially after two things happened at the end of August.

First, Chelsea signed Brazilian winger Willian from Shakhtar Donetsk for £30 million. That was a huge amount of money compared to the £7 million that The Blues had paid Genk for Kevin.

'There's no way *he's* going to sit on the bench,' Kevin muttered moodily. The last thing he, or Chelsea, needed was another skilful attacker.

Kevin's second setback came ahead of the UEFA Super Cup against Bayern Munich, his chance to win a first European trophy. He travelled out to Germany with his Chelsea teammates but two hours before kick-off, Mourinho gave him the bad news.

'I'm sorry but you're not in the matchday squad,' the manager explained.

Kevin couldn't believe it – he wasn't in the

starting line-up, and he wasn't even on the bench either! Instead, he had to watch the game from the stands, like a supporter, as Chelsea lost on penalties.

When the media asked Mourinho, his answer was simple: 'If De Bruyne doesn't play twenty games this season, it's because he doesn't deserve it.'

'He doesn't deserve it'? What had Kevin done to upset his manager so much? He didn't understand it; he always trained hard and played hard too.

'I'm not a troublemaker!' Kevin protested.

Kevin just wanted to play football. However, when he finally got another chance to play, against Swindon in the League Cup, it was clear that something was wrong. He couldn't get his head in the game. He looked lost out on the right wing and his creative spark was missing. To make matters worse, as he struggled, Juan and Willian shone.

Mourinho had seen enough. 'Kevin didn't convince me against Swindon, so he's out of the squad. He has to understand that Chelsea aren't Werder Bremen.'

The manager's public criticism left Kevin feeling

hurt and angry. His friends and family flew to London to comfort him.

'Forget about it, he's just testing you,' his dad, Herwig, told him. 'He wants you to show that amazing mental strength of yours!'

Kevin had lost his usual confidence, though. 'What if Mourinho is right?' he began to think. Maybe, he wasn't good enough...

'No, you *are* good enough!' his mum, Anna, told him. 'If you keep believing, you'll soon prove that you're Premier League quality!'

But how was Kevin supposed to prove himself when he wasn't on the pitch? Often, he wasn't even on the bench. When Chelsea travelled to Romania to play against Steaua Bucharest in the Champions League, Mourinho left Kevin behind to train with the youth team. It was so humiliating!

By November, Kevin had decided that he had no chance at Chelsea. He knew when he wasn't wanted. It was sad but true. His days at Stamford Bridge were numbered, before he had even scored a Premier League goal.

'Look, why don't you wait until the end of the season?' Eden suggested. He hated to see his friend looking so unhappy.

Kevin shook his head. He wasn't the kind of player who would sit around on the subs' bench and wait.

'Okay, well, why don't you ask to go out on loan for the rest of the season?'

Kevin shook his head again. Once he made up his mind, that was it. At the age of fourteen, he had made the bold move from Genk to Gent. Now, it was time to make another move and this one was even bolder. Kevin wanted to leave Chelsea, and not just for a few months. He was twenty-two years old and he wanted a permanent home. He wanted to go where he was wanted.

'Please let me go!' Kevin begged his manager.

Eventually, Mourinho accepted his request. 'Okay, leave it with me. We'll find you a new club.'

That new club wouldn't be another English club; Chelsea wouldn't allow that. Instead, Kevin was going back to Germany.

Klaus Allofs, the man behind his loan move to

Werder Bremen, was now the Sporting Director
of VfL Wolfsburg. 'The Wolves' had two good
goalscorers up front – Bas Dost and Ivica Olić – but
who was going to create chances for them? What
Wolfsburg wanted was a star playmaker to build
their team around, and Allofs knew the perfect
midfield magician – Kevin! £20 million seemed like a
lot of money but it would soon turn out to be a total
bargain.

Kevin was just pleased to be playing regular
football again. It took time for him to get his form
and confidence back but he ended the 2013–14
season with three goals and six assists.

'Next year, I'll be unstoppable!' he told his
teammate, Timm Klose.

Before that, however, Kevin was off to Brazil with
the Belgian national team. He couldn't wait to make
his World Cup dream come true.

CHAPTER 17

BELGIANS IN BRAZIL

The whole world was excited about the 2014 World Cup, but the Belgium fans were beyond excited. As the message on their red T-shirts read, 'We Are Ready!' After twelve frustrating years, they were back where they belonged, playing in football's biggest international competition again. Not only that, but Belgium also had a great chance of getting through the group stage this time. All they had to do was beat Algeria, Russia and South Korea.

'No problem, we can go all the way!' the nation hoped.

'We won't face Germany or Argentina until the quarter-finals!' Kevin hoped.

They couldn't get ahead of themselves, though. At international level, every match was difficult. Anyone could beat anyone, especially at the World Cup...

At half-time against Algeria, Belgium were losing 1–0. What an awful start! Eden, Kevin and Nacer had lots of possession but they were struggling to find that killer pass to the striker, Romelu Lukaku. Their heads hung low as they returned to the dressing room.

'Keep going!' Wilmots, their manager, urged. 'We've got forty-five minutes to turn this game around. That's plenty of time for a talented team like us!'

In the second half, Belgium battled back. Dries came on for Nacer and added even more speed to the attack. They were creating so many chances, but the ball just wouldn't go in.

'Come on, Belgium!' the fans groaned in the Estádio Mineirão in Belo Horizonte. They hadn't travelled all that way to watch their country lose to Algeria.

On the road to the World Cup, Kevin had saved the day so many times, with a goal or an assist, or sometimes even both. What could he do on football's biggest stage? At times like this, the top players always shone. He thought about his heroes. At World Cup 1998, Owen had scored a wondergoal for England against Argentina, and Zidane had scored two goals for France against Brazil in the final. It was Kevin's turn now.

With twenty minutes to go, he got the ball on the left wing. Should he pass, dribble or shoot? Divock Origi and Marouane Fellaini were waiting in the box, so Kevin curled in a dangerous cross. It was so accurate that Marouane didn't even have to jump. He just flicked a header up over the goalkeeper. 1–1!

Game on! Ten minutes later, Eden dribbled forward from his own half and slipped the ball across to Dries. Dries took a touch and then fired a shot into the roof of the net. 2–1 – *phew*, what a relief!

At the final whistle, the Belgium players, coaches and fans all hugged each other happily. They hadn't made life easy for themselves but they had their first victory.

'We've just got be patient!' Wilmots told his team.

'The chances will come.'

In the second match against Russia, Belgium didn't take their chance until the eighty-eighth minute. Eden skipped past two defenders and pulled the back for Divock to score. 1–0!

A lot of the players ran to celebrate with Divock, but Kevin hugged Eden instead. Belgium's two best players weren't rivals; they were teammates, and friends.

'That was world-class, mate – thanks to you, we're through!'

The Belgium players knew that they would need to play a lot better in the second round against the USA. The Americans had already knocked out Cristiano Ronaldo's Portugal and Michael Essien's Ghana. Kevin didn't want to be next.

'Come on, we've got to take our chances today!' He clapped and cheered before kick-off.

But Belgium couldn't because the USA goalkeeper, Tim Howard, was having the game of his life. He saved shots from Kevin, Divock, Eden and Kevin Mirallas. There was just no way through.

'Keep going!' Wilmots, their manager, urged, as the match went to extra-time.

Kevin certainly wasn't giving up. He wanted his first World Cup to last as long as possible. As Romelu dribbled into the penalty area, Kevin burst forward to support him, yelling 'Pass!' When the ball came to him, he cut past two tired defenders and steered his shot past Howard's outstretched leg and into the bottom corner.

Goooooooooooooooooooaaaaaaaaaaaaaaaalllllllllllll lllllllllllllll!!!!!!!!!!!!!!!!!!

Finally, Belgium had their breakthrough! Kevin ran towards the bench with his arms out wide. What a time to score his first-ever World Cup goal! It was a scene of total ecstasy – Wilmots was on the pitch, punching the air, and so were all the substitutes. Eden raced over to celebrate with Kevin.

'*That* was world-class!' he shouted over the deafening noise of the crowd.

But would that one goal be enough? A second would make them feel safer. Eden passed to Kevin, who threaded the ball through to Romelu.

Romelu's first-time shot thundered into the top corner. 2–0!

Surely, now they could relax and start the party? The fans thought so but the USA hit back quickly. They scored one and nearly scored another. It was a tense final ten minutes but Belgium held on for the victory.

'We did it!' Kevin cried out, throwing his arms up in the air.

Had he ever felt so much joy, relief and adrenaline at the same time? No, this was a very special moment. Belgium were through to the World Cup quarter-finals for the first time in twenty-eight years.

That was a great achievement but the Red Devils were about to face their toughest challenge yet. How would Kevin and Eden get on against Messi and co? Argentina had struggled past Switzerland but, with the best player in the world in their team, they were capable of anything.

In the eighth minute, Messi escaped from Kevin and Marouane in midfield. He passed to Ángel Di María, who passed to Gonzalo Higuaín, who smashed the ball into the bottom corner. 1–0 to Argentina!

'No, no, NO!' Kevin yelled out in frustration.

At least Belgium still had over eighty minutes to find an equaliser. That was plenty of time for a talented team like them. Unfortunately, however, their star players had run out of steam. Kevin's legs felt so heavy as he chased after the ball in the bright Brazilian sunshine. He did his best to find one more moment of magic but he had nothing left to give.

As the Argentina players celebrated, Kevin stared down at his feet and sighed. 'Not this time,' he thought to himself.

'You should be very proud of yourself,' Wilmots said, patting him on the back. 'For your first World Cup, you were fantastic!'

Kevin thanked his manager and then moved on to his next challenges: the Bundesliga title with Wolfsburg, Euro 2016, and then the big one – World Cup 2018.

CHAPTER 18

KING OF THE ASSISTS

As the 2014–15 club season kicked off, Kevin could tell it was going to be a special one. He felt settled at Wolfsburg and he was enjoying the freedom that his manager, Dieter Hecking, had given him. Just as he had done at Genk and Werder Bremen, Kevin was playing the beautiful game his way again.

In pre-season, he raced down the right wing and crossed for Nicklas Bendtner to score. *GOAL!* Nicklas lifted Kevin high into the air.

'You're the King of the Assists!' he cheered.

Kevin loved that nickname but his mind was focused on the big team trophies – the Bundesliga title, the German Cup and the Europa League. Why couldn't The Wolves challenge for all three at the same time? Anything was possible now that they had the King of the Assists in their midfield.

By Christmas, Kevin already had fourteen assists in all competitions, plus a real contender for goal of the season.

In the Europa League against Lille, Wolfsburg were 1–0 down with ten minutes to go. As Ricardo Rodríguez took the corner, Kevin waited on the edge of the box for the rebound. A Lille defender headed the ball away but straight towards Kevin. He took one step towards it and struck a fierce right-foot volley. The technique was out of this world, like Zidane in the 2002 Champions League final. The ball flew through the crowded penalty area and into the top corner.

Goooooooooooooooooooaaaaaaaaaaaaaaaaallllllllllll llllllllllllll!!!!!!!!!!!!!!!!!!!

It was an absolute wonder-strike and a game-saver for Wolfsburg. Yet Kevin just wagged his finger and high-fived his teammate, Vieirinha. No smile, no big deal! He was a man on a mission.

At the winter break, Wolfsburg were still

challenging for all three trophies. They were second in the Bundesliga and still going strong in the German Cup and the Europa League too. Thanks to Kevin's creative genius, the dream was still alive.

But Pep Guardiola at Bayern Munich was so impressed by Kevin's performances that he tried to sign him during the January transfer window. Bayern Munich were the biggest club in Germany and one of the biggest clubs in the world. Who wouldn't want to play for them? Kevin. He decided that he wasn't yet ready to make another big move.

'It's too soon,' he told his friend Timm. 'I've only been here a year and I'm enjoying myself!'

Kevin was also worried that joining Bayern Munich could be another mistake like Chelsea. Guardiola already had amazing attackers like Franck Ribéry, Arjen Robben, Mario Götze, Thomas Müller and Robert Lewandowski in his squad. Did he really need Kevin as well? That was just plain greedy!

'No way am I going somewhere to warm the bench again,' he told himself.

At Wolfsburg, Kevin was the star man and that

was the role that he was born to play. When Bayern arrived at the Volkswagen Arena, he treated them to one of his best-ever midfield masterclasses.

Kevin burst through the middle and set up Bas Dost to score. 1–0!

After that assist, Kevin switched from goal-maker to goal-scorer. Maximilian Arnold played a great pass through the Bayern defence, and Kevin was through on goal, with just Manuel Neuer to beat.

Gooooooooooooaaaaaaaaaalllllllllllllllllllll!!!!!!!!!!!!!

3–0! Kevin stood in front of the delighted Wolfsburg fans with his arms up in the air. He loved being their hero.

De Bruyne! De Bruyne! De Bruyne!

Twenty minutes later, Kevin sprinted towards goal again. As he dribbled into the penalty area, Bayern's centre-back, Dante, stood in his way. Kevin didn't have a weaker foot, just two magic wands. Which way would he go? He cut inside on his right and faked to shoot. With Dante fooled, he rolled the ball across to his left. *Abracadabra!* With one strike of the boot, Kevin found the top corner.

Gooooooooooooaaaaaaaaaallllllllllllllllllllll!!!!!!!!!!!!

4–1! Wolfsburg hadn't just beaten Bayern; they had *thrashed* them.

'Kev, I'm so glad you stayed!' Timm cried out as The Wolves celebrated a famous victory. 'What would we do without you?'

The Wolfsburg fans didn't even want to think about that. Kevin was a superstar now, the King of the Assists. Against his old club Werder Bremen, he got a hat-trick of them.

Kevin crossed for Maximilian head home. 2–2!

Kevin played the perfect pass to leave Bas with a simple finish. 3–3!

Kevin set up Bas again with a teasing ball. 4–3!

Bas ran towards Kevin with a huge grin on his face. 'Man, you make my life so easy!' he screamed.

Kevin was in the best form of his life. Every single touch felt so easy and looked so classy. In the Europa League against Inter Milan, he glided around the pitch like Zidane. First, Kevin passed the ball into the net and then he curled a swerving free kick into the bottom corner.

'What were Chelsea thinking when they let you go?' Hecking joked. 'Mourinho must be a madman!'

In the end, Napoli knocked Wolfsburg out in the quarter-finals but Kevin still had plenty left to play for in other competitions. His goals and assists helped The Wolves to finish second in the Bundesliga behind Bayern Munich.

'We'll be playing in the Champions League next year!' Kevin cried out joyfully.

Wolfsburg even had the chance to finish their terrific season with a trophy. In the final of the German Cup, they faced Borussia Dortmund, the team that had tried to buy Kevin from Chelsea back in 2013. Jürgen Klopp had failed and 'the one that got away' came back to haunt him in Berlin.

The score was 1–1 when Daniel Caligiuri laid the ball back to Kevin. He was a long way out to shoot but why not? He had the confidence, the power *and* the technique. *Bang!* It wasn't one of Kevin's sweetest strikes, but the ball bobbled all the way into the bottom corner.

Goooooooooooaaaaaaaaaallllllllllllllllllllll!!!!!!!!!!!!!

Kevin held up the badge on his Wolfsburg shirt and pointed to it. After his dark days at Chelsea, the club had offered him a second chance. The Wolves had believed in him and welcomed him into their pack. The fans loved him and he loved them right back.

'That's for you!' Kevin told them.

On the sideline, Klopp just shook his head and sighed. 'If only...'

At the full-time whistle, Wolfsburg were the German Cup winners for the first time ever. What a moment! Up on the stage, Kevin jumped up and down with his teammates, enjoying an incredible end to an incredible season.

Ten goals, twenty-seven assists and a team trophy – not bad for a Chelsea flop! And he wasn't finished yet. He picked up the Bundesliga Player of the Year award too, ahead of Neuer and Lewandowski.

Kevin had found the perfect way, and the perfect place, to prove people wrong. He was now the King of the Assists and one of the best playmakers in the world.

CHAPTER 19

PREMIER LEAGUE RETURN

'I got an offer from Manchester City,' Kevin told Timm after pre-season training one day. He made it sound so normal, like a phone call from his mum. 'What do you think?'

Timm seemed more excited than his friend. 'I think that if it was me, I would go there as fast as I could. I would even swim there if I had to!'

City had just finished second in the Premier League, eight points behind Kevin's old club Chelsea. That wasn't good enough, and so manager Manuel Pellegrini was looking to rebuild his team with some top new attackers. Young English winger Raheem Sterling had already joined Sergio Agüero, David

Silva and Yaya Touré. Would Kevin be next?

'You'll play lots of matches here, I promise,' Vincent, his Belgian teammate, tried to persuade him. 'It'll be so much fun! Plus, you've got unfinished business in England, haven't you?'

He was right; Kevin did have a point to prove in the Premier League. He knew that he wasn't just a Chelsea flop, but English football fans didn't. Yet. And City were now one of the best clubs in Europe…

First, however, the two clubs had to agree a transfer fee. £40 million? Rejected! £47 million? Rejected!

'We'll do everything we can to keep De Bruyne,' Wolfsburg's Sporting Director told the media.

City weren't giving up, though, and they returned with a third and final offer of £58 million. There was no way that the German club could say no to that kind of money.

The deal was done, making Kevin the second most expensive signing in Premier League history. There was a lot of pressure on him to perform well but that didn't worry him. He had learnt a lot since his last spell in England. He was a different player now – older, wiser, and a whole lot better.

'I want to reach the highest level possible as a player,' Kevin told the English newspapers. 'That's why I've come to City and hopefully we can win lots of trophies.'

He started as a substitute against Crystal Palace but after twenty-five minutes, Sergio picked up an injury and had to come off.

'Kevin, get ready!' a City coach shouted suddenly.

Great, he was bored on the bench already! As Kevin quickly changed out of his coat and tracksuit, the coach talked him through the team tactics. He was still pulling his '17 DE BRUYNE' shirt over his head as he high-fived Sergio on the touchline.

'Go out there and create some magic,' Pellegrini told him. 'Enjoy yourself!'

Kevin looked calm and focused as he ran onto the pitch, folding down his shirt collar. It felt good to be back in the Premier League. Could he make an instant impact? He exchanged some nice passes with Samir Nasri and Jesús Navas but without their star striker, City were struggling to score.

'Come on, keep going!' Kevin shouted to his new teammates. He was determined to win on his debut.

With five minutes to go, Kelechi Iheanacho finally tapped in a rebound to make it 1– 0. *Phew!* It hadn't been one of Kevin's best midfield masterclasses, but City had the three points and that was all that mattered.

'Well played, mate,' Vincent congratulated him at full-time. 'It's great to have you here!'

Kevin was soon firing at full speed and he scored in his next three games in a row. By the time Newcastle arrived at the Etihad Stadium, Sergio and David were back and so City's talented new trio tore them to shreds.

Kevin passed to David, who passed to Sergio, who cut inside and blasted the ball into the bottom corner. 2–1!

Kevin split the Newcastle defence with one of his perfect passes and Sergio cheekily chipped the keeper. 3–1!

Kevin was feeling super chilled and super

confident. As the cross came towards him, he struck it first time on the volley. His technique was as brilliant as ever. The ball looped up over the keeper's arms and into the net.

Gooooooooooooooooooooaaaaaaaaaaaaaaaaallllllllllll llllllllllllll!!!!!!!!!!!!!!!!!!!

4–1! It was another Zidane special, a strike that Kevin had been practising since he was a young boy in Belgium. The City fans behind the goal jumped to their feet with joy. They had a new hero to sing about.

Ohhhhhhhh! Kevin De Bruyne!

Ohhhhhhhh! Kevin De Bruyne!

And there were more goals to come. David played a brilliant ball forward to Sergio, who curled the ball into the bottom corner again. 5–1!

As he received the pass from David, Kevin was off balance but he still managed to cross the ball with his left foot to give Sergio an easy tap-in at the back post. 6–1!

'You guys are the best!' Sergio cheered, hugging his two favourite teammates.

Kevin was really enjoying his return to the Premier League. Sometimes he played on the left wing, sometimes he played on the right wing, and sometimes he played through the middle. But wherever he played, Kevin gave 110 per cent effort for his new club.

He was also enjoying his return to the Champions League. With seconds to go against Sevilla, Yaya dribbled forward for one last attack. It was 1–1 and he had Kevin to his right and Raheem to his left. Who would he choose to be City's matchwinner?

Kevin! When the pass arrived, he dribbled at the full-back, tempting him to make a silly tackle. He didn't, so Kevin rolled the ball from his right foot to his left foot and skidded a shot into the bottom corner.

Goooooooooooooooooooaaaaaaaaaaaaaaaalllllllllllll llllllllllllll!!!!!!!!!!!!!!!!!!!!

'Come on!' he roared, punching the air.

'At least give us a smile, mate!' Yaya teased.

Kevin was enjoying his return to the League Cup too. During his difficult days at Chelsea, he had struggled against Swindon. Two years later, he was scoring four goals in three games, as he led City past Sunderland, Crystal Palace and Hull. Kevin found the net in the semi-final against Everton too, but his night ended in disaster. As he tried to shield the ball from Ramiro Funes Mori, he felt a shooting pain in his right knee. 'Arghhhh!' he cried out as he fell to the floor.

It didn't look too bad but Kevin knew that it was serious straight away. As the match continued, he rolled around in agony and floods of tears. The Everton goalkeeper Joel Robles tried to help him up, but that was impossible.

'Ref!' Joel shouted. 'He needs a physio!'

The pain became unbearable. 'Stop!' Kevin signalled when the team doctor tried to lift his right leg. He left the field on a stretcher and the worried fans clapped him all the way down the tunnel. Was Kevin's season over already? It was definitely the worst injury of his career, but he focused on recovering as quickly as possible.

'We need you!' Vincent said to give his friend some extra motivation.

Kevin missed City's League Cup final win over Liverpool, the club he had supported as a child, but he made it back in time to save his team in their Champions League quarter-final against PSG.

In the first leg in France, Kevin scored in a 2–2 draw. Those two away goals gave City the advantage, but they still had work to do at the Etihad. Could they really keep PSG's world-class attackers Zlatan Ibrahimović, Ángel Di María and Edinson Cavani quiet for ninety minutes? Another City goal would really help to settle everyone's jangling nerves...

With fifteen minutes to go, Fernandinho laid the ball back to Kevin on the edge of the area. The City fans held their breath – was this the big moment they'd been waiting for? It was certainly the moment Kevin had been waiting for, but he didn't panic under the pressure. Instead, he tricked Cavani with a drop of the shoulder and then curled an incredible shot past the goalkeeper.

Goooooooooooooooooooaaaaaaaaaaaaaaaalllllllllllll llllllllllllll!!!!!!!!!!!!!!!!!!!

Kevin still didn't smile but he did celebrate his crucial strike with a knee slide. After all, City were going through, thanks to him.

'What a beauty!' Fernandinho screamed, hugging his team's hero tightly.

Ohhhhhhhh! Kevin De Bruyne!

Ohhhhhhhh! Kevin De Bruyne!

Would he ever get tired of hearing 50,000 fans chanting his name? No, never – it was the best feeling in the world!

That turned out to be the highlight of Kevin's excellent first season at Manchester City, as they lost to Real Madrid in the Champions League semi-finals and finished fourth in the Premier League.

'We can do much better than that!' Vincent groaned.

Kevin agreed. He was pleased with his performances but he now felt ready to reach the next level. Sixteen goals and fifteen assists on his Premier League return – not bad for a Chelsea flop! He won City's Player of the Year award but how high could he go?

City were replacing Pellegrini with Pep Guardiola, the former Barcelona and Bayern Munich boss. Playing in his best position, and coached by the best manager in the business, could Kevin finally become 'the new Zidane', the best midfielder in the world?

Yes, he could, and he would! Kevin didn't doubt himself for a second.

CHAPTER 20

EURO 2016

After their encouraging World Cup experience, Belgium's golden generation qualified for Euro 2016 with ease. Kevin and Eden scored five goals each to lead their country to France.

'We're one of the best teams in Europe now!' Kevin argued and the football world agreed. Germany were the favourites to win the tournament, then France, then Spain, then Belgium! Why not? The Red Devils certainly had the talent; now, they just needed the belief to go with it.

'At our best, we can beat anyone!' Wilmots kept telling his players.

Their group, Group E, was one of the toughest

in the tournament. Belgium had to take on Italy, Republic of Ireland and Sweden. There would be no easy games this time.

'Come on lads, let's win this!' Eden clapped and cheered before their first match against Italy.

But Belgium didn't win; they lost. In attack, they wasted great chances to score and in defence, they made massive mistakes to throw the game away. At the final whistle, Kevin wandered around the pitch in shock and despair. What a poor performance by the team, but especially by him! He had barely touched the ball. Yes, he was tired after a long season at City but that was no excuse. He had to do better.

Wilmots the manager put an arm around Kevin's shoulder and tried to lift his spirits. 'Today was a bad day, but if we win our next two games, we'll still go through. It's not over yet!'

Kevin nodded glumly. He had worked so hard to become one of Belgium's big game players but unless he upped his game, he could find himself back on the bench.

For the second match against Republic of Ireland,

Wilmots moved Kevin from the right wing to the middle. That was his favourite position to play because he had the freedom to do what he did best – create chances for his teammates.

CHANCE! Kevin delivered a dangerous cross into the box but Eden smashed it high over the bar.

CHANCE! Kevin chipped a brilliant through-ball to Yannick Carrasco but the goalkeeper made a great save.

CHANCE! Kevin passed to Thomas Meunier but his shot trickled wide.

CHANCE! Kevin curled a corner straight onto Toby Alderweireld's head but a defender cleared it off the goal-line.

'Come on, we have to take one of these chances!' Kevin complained.

Early in the second half, he passed to Romelu on the edge of the penalty area. This time, Romelu took his time to get the shot just right. GOAL – 1–0!

'That's more like it!' Kevin screamed as the whole team celebrated together.

Once Belgium scored one, they soon scored two

more. A 3–0 victory helped to build their confidence back up again.

'We can do this!' Vincent cheered.

With a win against Sweden, the Red Devils could qualify for the second round of Euro 2016. But as the minutes ticked by, that task got trickier and trickier. As hard as Kevin and Eden tried, Belgium just could not get the ball over the goal-line!

'Keep going!' Wilmots called out from the touchline.

Just when they were beginning to give up hope, Radja Nainggolan hit a long-range rocket into the top corner. GOAL – 1–0!

As he watched the ball land in the back of the net, Kevin threw his arms up in the air. *Phew*, what a relief! He turned to the fans behind the goal and clenched his fists.

'Come on!' he roared.

They may have beaten Sweden, but if they were going to win Euro 2016, Belgium had a lot of work to do in the knockout stages, starting with beating Hungary in Toulouse. With Kevin in their team, they knew that they would always get chances to score, but they had to be better at taking them. In the tenth minute, he whipped another dangerous delivery into the box and this time, no-one could stop Toby's header.

'Hey, stay focused!' Vincent warned the players as they jumped on Toby.

Kevin nearly made it 2–0 with a fantastic free kick but the goalkeeper tipped it onto the crossbar. So close! In the end, Belgium had to wait nearly seventy minutes to secure their victory.

Eden dribbled down the left wing and crossed to Michy Batshuayi. 2–0!

Eden got the ball again and set off on a brilliant solo run. 3–0!

Radja threaded a pass through to Yannick. 4–0!

Suddenly, Belgium were on fire! 'What about me?' Kevin joked. He was now their only attacker who hadn't scored at the tournament.

'Don't worry, you're our playmaker,' Michy laughed. 'You create and we finish!'

England were out, Spain were out, and Germany

were taking on Italy. Surely, Belgium wouldn't get a better chance to lift the trophy. The semi-finals were in sight but first, they had to get past the surprise team of Euro 2016, Wales. They were playing with lots of spirit and confidence, and they had Gareth Bale and Aaron Ramsey in attack.

'I don't want to see any silly mistakes tonight,' Wilmots warned his players. 'You need to show one hundred per cent concentration from start to finish!'

With their manager's words ringing in their ears, Belgium attacked brilliantly at the beginning. Eden passed to Radja and he hit another long-range rocket. GOAL – 1–0!

'What a strike!' Kevin screamed. 'What a start!'

As Wales battled back, Belgium needed to stay calm and focused. 'No silly mistakes!' their manager had told them, but at the crucial moment, they switched off. They left Ashley Williams unmarked at a corner and he headed the ball powerfully towards goal. Kevin was on the goal-line but he couldn't keep it out.

1–1: game on! Could Belgium take the lead

again? Eden and Romelu both had chances but they couldn't hit the target.

'Keep going!' Wilmots called out from the touchline.

As Ramsey crossed from the right, Hal Robson-Kanu had his back to goal and two Belgium defenders to beat. But he fooled them both with one clever turn and shot past Thibaut Courtois. 2–1 to Wales!

The Belgium fans in the stadium looked stunned and so did the players.

'How did we let that happen?' Kevin screamed at his teammates.

'Come on, we've still got plenty of time to turn this around!' Eden called out, trying to stay positive.

Belgium needed their star playmaker to take control of the game, but Kevin was struggling. His legs felt as heavy as sandbags as he ran from box to box. Instead, the team turned to Plan B – long balls to the big guys, Romelu and Marouane.

That nearly worked but it just wasn't Belgium's day. Wales went up the other end and scored again. 3–1: game over!

At the final whistle, Kevin stood with his hands on his hips, staring up at the empty stands. The heartbroken Belgium fans had gone home already. Their team had let them down. How had they lost to Wales? It was so embarrassing, humiliating.

The quarter-finals of World Cup 2014 and the quarter-finals of Euro 2016 – it was good but not good enough. Kevin knew that Belgium couldn't afford to waste any more chances. World Cup 2018 would have to be their tournament.

CHAPTER 21

THE PEP REVOLUTION

'It will be hard for me to play the way I like to play in the Premier League but we did it at Barcelona and we did it at Bayern Munich. They say it won't be possible in England and I just say, okay, let's try!'

Pep Guardiola had a grand plan for Manchester City. He wanted his new team to play passing, flowing football and for that, Kevin would be crucial. He would no longer be playing out wide on the wing, though. He was now Pep's main man in the middle.

'This is the best news ever!' Kevin cried out. He couldn't wait to make the most of his creative freedom.

In the big Manchester derby against United, he was City's man of the match. After fifteen minutes, Kevin flicked the ball cleverly past Daley Blind and then shot calmly past David de Gea.

Goooooooooooooooooooooaaaaaaaaaaaaaaaalllllllllllll llllllllllllllll!!!!!!!!!!!!!!!!!!!!!!

Twenty minutes later, he beat Blind again in the box with a beautiful turn. His shot struck the post but Kelechi was there to tap in the rebound. 2–0!

The City fans went absolutely wild at Old Trafford. What an important win! Kevin was already a club hero but now he was a club *super*hero.

Ohhhhhhhh! Kevin De Bruyne!

Ohhhhhhhh! Kevin De Bruyne!

A week later, Kevin tormented Bournemouth with another magical midfield masterclass. He stood over the free kick and waited for the wall to jump. When they did, he shot underneath their feet and into the bottom corner. 1–0!

Kevin burst forward on the counter-attack. He passed right to Raheem, who passed left to Kelechi. 2–0!

Kevin burst forward on another counter-attack.

This time, he passed left to Kelechi, who passed right to Raheem. 3–0!

Kevin played a perfect pass between two defenders to find İlkay Gündoğan in space. 4–0!

The Bournemouth players just stood there, looking at each other for answers:

How did he just do that?

What planet is he from?

What can we do to stop him?

'De Bruyne is one of the best players I've ever worked with,' the City manager told the media after the match.

Wow! Kevin beamed with pride when he heard those words. Guardiola had worked with superstars like Andrés Iniesta, Xavi and Messi! That was the world-class level that he was aiming for. With his manager's support and belief, Kevin knew that he could get there. He wasn't scoring as many goals as before but he was now England's King of the Assists.

During the 2015–16 campaign, Kevin had set up nine Premier League goals. That put him just inside the Top Ten but he was a long way behind the other top playmakers like Arsenal's Mesut Özil and Tottenham's Christian Eriksen.

'I can do much better than that!' Kevin told himself. He was always setting himself new targets, and competing against the best players in the game.

During the 2016–17 campaign, Kevin reached ten assists before March had even started. His passes were so clever and so perfect – the right angle, the right speed, the right place, the right time.

He threaded a teasing pass through three defenders to pick out Sergio at the front post. GOAL!

'Thanks, Kev!'

He played a long diagonal ball, from left to right, to set Raheem free. GOAL!

'Thanks, Kev!'

He chipped a clever cross, over Sergio and over Raheem, to Pablo Zabaleta at the back post. GOAL!

'Thanks, Kev!'

With his right foot and his left foot, in big games and small games, Kevin always created chances for his teammates. Often, he already had his next pass planned out in his head. If not, he lifted his head up, looking for the gaps in the defence, and the spaces in behind.

'Mate, you're like Superman,' Raheem told Kevin. 'No seriously, you've got X-ray vision!'

On the sidelines, Guardiola clapped and smiled. With Kevin driving his team forward from midfield, he was sure that he could achieve his English dream; he could play the way he liked to play and still win the Premier League title.

It didn't happen in that season, however. It was Chelsea who lifted England's top trophy. The Blues finished a massive fifteen points ahead of City.

'This was our warm-up,' Guardiola comforted his frustrated players. 'Next year, we'll win it!'

And in the Champions League, Kevin scored a swerving free kick in a brilliant 3–1 win over Pep's old team Barcelona. However, in the next round, City came unstuck against Monaco. They attacked brilliantly but they defended terribly.

'We lose and we learn,' Guardiola told his disappointed team. 'Next year, we'll come back stronger!'

Pep ended his first Premier League season, 2016–17, trophy-less. City didn't even have a shiny cup to show for all their beautiful, flowing football. They lost to Arsenal in the semi-finals of the FA Cup, and to Manchester United in the fourth round of the League Cup. Were the critics right? Was it impossible to win the Guardiola way in England?

No, nothing could make him give up on his grand plan. The Pep Revolution had started but it would take some time. His City team was like a puzzle where only half of the pieces fitted perfectly. Pep had his centrepiece – Kevin! Now, he just needed to complete the puzzle by finding the missing pieces to fit around him...

Kevin was more than satisfied with his second season at City. Under Guardiola's guidance, he could feel himself getting better and better. He finished top of the Premier League Assists chart with eighteen. That was nine more than Özil and three more than Eriksen.

Kevin had lots of reasons to feel confident about his footballing future at City. 'Next year, we're going to be unstoppable!' he declared.

CHAPTER 22

ROAD TO THE WORLD CUP 2018

After the disappointment of Euro 2016, Belgium decided that it was time for another change. They had so many brilliant footballers, so why weren't they working well together? Kevin at Manchester City, Eden at Chelsea, and Romelu at Everton; they were all starring for their clubs but not yet for their country. Why not?

'We need a better tactical plan!' argued some fans.

'We need more team spirit!' argued others.

Maybe a new manager could lead Belgium to glory. So, out went Wilmots and in came Roberto Martínez.

'Trust me, he's good!' Romelu told his teammates.

He had worked with Martínez at Everton.

The new manager also brought former France star Thierry Henry with him as his assistant. It was a really exciting time for Belgian football. Could Martínez and Henry take the team all the way to the top?

Their first job was to lead the nation to the 2018 World Cup in Russia. That task looked fairly straightforward. Surely, they could top Group H above Greece, Bosnia and Herzegovina, Estonia, Cyprus and Gibraltar?

Martínez kept the core of the team the same – Thibaut in goal, Toby and Jan in defence, Axel in midfield and Kevin, Eden and Romelu in attack. But what about Dries? He was scoring goals for fun at Napoli. There was no way that they could leave him on the bench. How could they fit him into the team too?

At first, it was easy. Kevin missed the matches against Bosnia and Herzegovina and Gibraltar through injury. Dries played instead and Belgium won, respectively, 4–0 and then 6–0. But when

Kevin returned for the game against Estonia,
Martínez had a decision to make.

'What if we drop Kevin a bit deeper?' the manager
wondered. 'He's quick, he's strong and he can tackle
when he needs to!'

With Kevin playing alongside Axel in midfield,
Belgium would then have space for Eden, Romelu
and Dries. It was a line-up dominated by attackers,
but it was worth a try. Poor Estonia didn't stand
a chance.

Kevin played a long diagonal pass to Yannick
Carrasco on the left. He crossed the ball and Thomas
Meunier headed in at the back post. 1–0!

Kevin passed a free kick across to Dries, and his
shot was deflected past the goalkeeper. 2–0!

Romelu chested the ball down to Dries, who set
up Eden to score. 3–0!

After Estonia managed to pull back a goal, Dries
slipped it through to Romelu, who crossed to
Yannick. 4–1!

Kevin played a great one-two with Dries and his
cross was deflected past the goalkeeper. 5–1!

Dries lobbed the keeper. 6–1!

Kevin burst forward and passed to Thomas. His cross eventually came to Romelu, who made no mistake. 7–1!

Five minutes later, Romelu ran through and scored again. 8–1!

On the touchline, Martínez clapped and smiled. Belgium's new line-up was working brilliantly together.

Out on the pitch, Kevin was smiling too. He was having fun in his new role. It really suited him. No, he hadn't scored any of his team's goals but he had started almost every attack. When he got the ball in central midfield, he had more options to pass to, and more space to pick out that perfect pass. That was Kevin's favourite thing.

'This is it, boys!' Eden said excitedly. 'Russia, here we come!'

Belgium raced along the road to the 2018 World Cup. With a 2–1 win away in Greece, they became the first European nation to qualify. Kevin and his teammates didn't celebrate in the same wild way they had four years earlier, but they still linked arms and ran over to take a bow in front of the fans.

Allez la Belgique! Allez la Belgique!

They had won nine out of their ten matches, scoring a massive forty-three goals. That was a new European record! According to the FIFA rankings, Belgium were now the third best team in the world.

They couldn't get ahead of themselves, though. The real test would come at the main event in Russia. The nation had great expectations for their Red Devils this time. Could Belgium finally defeat the top teams in international football – Brazil, Argentina, Germany, Spain, Portugal, France?

Kevin couldn't wait to play in his second World Cup. In his new midfield role, he was ready to lead his nation forward to glory.

CHAPTER 23

TROPHY TIME

When Pep Guardiola saw Kevin playing in that deeper midfield role for Belgium, he thought, 'Great idea – let's play him there for City too!'

There were already four fantastic attackers in the team: Sergio, Raheem, Gabriel Jesus and Leroy Sané. Once they got the ball, they had the speed and skill to destroy defences, but how were they going to get the ball in the first place? That's where Kevin came into Pep's grand plan. With his X-ray vision and his magical feet, he could pick out the perfect pass every time.

'Come on, we have to win the Premier League this season!' Kevin told his teammates. They couldn't settle for second best again, especially not against his old club, Chelsea.

City took a few games to find their best form, but once they did, they taught Liverpool a painful lesson at the Etihad. It was a joy to watch, and Kevin was at the centre of everything against his favourite childhood team.

Kevin ran and ran, from box to box, starting attack after attack. When the ball fell to him in central midfield, he already knew what he was going to do next. His brain worked so quickly and so did his feet. In a flash, he slid a smooth pass between the centre-backs for Sergio to run on to and score. 1–0!

'Thanks, mate!' Sergio cheered.

Kevin turned up on the right wing and curled a dangerous cross into the six-yard box for Gabriel to head home. 2–0! But no, the linesman's flag was up. Offside, goal disallowed!

Kevin turned up on the left wing and curled another dangerous cross into the six-yard box. Gabriel headed home again and this time, the flag stayed down. *Now* it was 2–0!

'Thanks, mate!' Gabriel cheered.

Was Pep's puzzle now complete? Not necessarily, but City were still on fire! After thrashing Liverpool 5–0, they thrashed Watford 6–0...

De Bruyne with pace on the delivery... it's a sensational goal from Agüero!

...then Crystal Palace 5–0...

De Bruyne plays it out to Sané on the left, who crosses to Sterling at the back post. GOAL!

What a pass that it is from De Bruyne to Agüero... Sterling taps in!

...then Stoke City 7–2!

De Bruyne through to Sané... Sterling scores! This looks like fantasy football!

De Bruyne to Sané again – another goal! They are just remarkable!

Kevin was supplying so many amazing assists, but what about some goals of his own?

Against Arsenal, he played a one-two with Fernandinho and kept running towards the penalty area. The defenders backed away, giving him lots of space to shoot. Why? Had Arsenal forgotten that Kevin was a really good goalscorer, as well as an awesome playmaker? He reminded them by slamming a powerful left foot shot into the bottom corner.

Goooooooooooooooooooaaaaaaaaaaaaaaaallllllllllll lllllllllllllll!!!!!!!!!!!!!!!!!!

'What a strike!' Leroy shouted as he chased after his teammate.

Kevin's next goal in the next game against Leicester City was even better. He thumped the ball into the top corner from outside the box.

Goooooooooooooooooooaaaaaaaaaaaaaaaallllllllllll lllllllllllllll!!!!!!!!!!!!!!!!!!

The fans couldn't get enough of their brilliant Belgian, their midfield maestro, their phenomenal playmaker:

Ohhhhhhhh! Kevin De Bruyne!

Ohhhhhhhh! Kevin De Bruyne!

He was now the best player in the Premier League and Manchester City were the best team too. By Christmas, they were already thirteen points clear at the top of the table.

'The title race is over!' the newspapers declared.

City didn't just relax, however. They couldn't, because they were challenging for not one, not two, not three, but FOUR top trophies!

In the Champions League, they flew through the group stage. Kevin set up two goals against Napoli and scored himself against Shakhtar Donetsk.

In the FA Cup, Kevin scored a free kick against Cardiff to lead his team into the fifth round.

In the League Cup, Kevin got two goals and an assist to lead his team past Bristol City and into the final.

Could City go on to win The Treble, or even The Quadruple? As long as their brilliant Belgian playmaker was fit and firing, anything seemed possible.

In February 2018, City's four-trophy quest dropped down to three. They were knocked out of the FA Cup by Wigan Athletic, but could they bounce back to beat Arsenal in the League Cup final?

'Come on, let's do this!' their captain, Vincent, called out in the dressing room.

Kevin didn't need any extra motivation. He was so determined to win his first Manchester City trophy at Wembley, the home of football. For once, he wasn't his team's hero, but he did get his wish.

In the first-half, Sergio lobbed the keeper to give them the lead. 1–0!

In the second-half, Vincent steered İlkay Gündoğan's shot into the net. 2–0!

David Silva sealed the victory with a great finish. 3–0!

At the final whistle, Kevin threw his arms up in the air. City were the League Cup winners! At last, it was trophy time.

'We did it!' he cried out as he jumped up and down with Vincent.

After collecting his winners' medal, Kevin took his turn to lift the shiny, silver trophy. What an incredible feeling!

But after a night of celebrations, it was back to business. One down, two trophies to go.

In the Champions League, City thrashed Basel 5–2 to set up a quarter-final against... Liverpool!

'Ah, not again!' Raheem groaned. He had left Liverpool to join City and their fans never let him forget that.

'Hey, it's fine, we can beat them again!' Kevin argued.

It was the most exciting match of the season so far. Which amazing manager would lead his team to victory: Jürgen Klopp or Pep Guardiola? And which of the Premier League's top two superstars would be the hero: Liverpool's Egyptian King Mohamed Salah or Kevin, City's King of the Assists?

City had to stay positive, especially in the first leg away at Anfield. The atmosphere was electric but not when City had the ball.

'Booooooooooooooooooooooooooooooooo!' the Kop End called out every time they touched it.

Unfortunately, Liverpool's strikeforce had too much speed and skill for the City defence. Salah, Sadio Mané and Roberto Firmino were simply unstoppable. By half-time, Pep's team were already 3–0 down. What a disastrous defeat! Could City bounce back from that?

'If we want to go through, we're going to need something special,' Kevin told the media.

In the second leg at the Etihad, City started strongly. Gabriel scored an early goal to make it 3–1 on aggregate.

'Come on, we can do this!' Kevin cheered.

He moved all over the pitch, from the left wing to the middle and then over to the right wing. He was desperate to create a moment of magic, that 'something special' for his team.

CHANCE! Kevin played a long diagonal pass to Bernardo Silva but his shot curled wide.

CHANCE! Kevin chipped a pass through to Leroy and he bundled the ball into the net. However, the linesman's flag was up – offside!

'No way!' the City players protested.

It was a bad decision but all they could do was play on. They needed two goals and there wasn't much time left.

'Attack!' Pep shouted from the sidelines. 'Attack!'

But in the second half, Liverpool caught them out on the counter-attack. Salah made it 4–2 and then

Firmino made it 5–2. It was game over for City and
Kevin was furious. Remember – on his list of least
favourite things, losing was right at the top.

'We have to stop making so many silly mistakes!'
Kevin snarled at his teammates.

He always wanted to win and he didn't care
who he had to shout at to make that happen.
Sadly, it was too little too late. City were out of the
Champions League.

The only thing that could cheer Kevin up was the
Premier League title. City were so close but they had
to stay strong and keep on winning. That's exactly
what they did, with a 3–1 victory at Tottenham.

'Brilliant, boys!' Guardiola cheered. 'We're nearly
there now!'

In fact, they won the title the very next day. Their
local rivals, Manchester United, lost to West Brom
and that was it – City were the Premier League
Champions!

Kevin watched the Manchester United match at
home with his family. At the final whistle, he jumped
off the sofa and punched the air. City had secured

the title with five games to spare.

'Unbelievable season for us,' he wrote to his Instagram followers. 'Very happy to call us champions this year.'

The real celebrations took place after their next home game, a 5–0 drubbing of Swansea City. Kevin and his teammates put on special shirts with '18 CHAMPIONS' on the back. As Vincent lifted the trophy, everyone bounced up and down together – the players, the coaches, the manager.

Campiones, Campiones, Olé! Olé! Olé!

It had been one huge team effort. The players thanked Guardiola by lifting him up and throwing him high into the air.

'Okay, enough, put me down now!' their manager begged. 'Please!'

After the fun and the fireworks, it was time for their families to join them. Kevin walked around the pitch with his girlfriend Michèle and their young son Mason in his arms. What shirt was he wearing? A Manchester City shirt, of course, with '17 DE BRUYNE' on the back!

'Hey, that's mine!' Kevin joked as Mason played with the winners' medal around his neck.

With four more games to go, City had nothing left to play for, except pleasure, pride and Premier League records. That was more than enough motivation to keep the team going. They finished with the most points, the most wins and the most goals in English history.

'We're the best!' Kevin cheered. 'Ever!'

On the final day of the season, he was still fighting for one last award. Salah was named the PFA Player of the Year, but Kevin's favourite prize was still up for grabs – the Premier League Playmaker of the Season award. With one game to go, he was tied with his teammate, Leroy, on fifteen assists.

'I have to win this!' Kevin thought to himself. He was so competitive about everything.

In the last minute against Southampton, he played an incredible long pass from deep in his own half. The ball flew over the defence and landed right at Gabriel's feet. Gabriel ran into the penalty area and lobbed the goalkeeper. GOAL – 1–0!

Assist Number Sixteen – Kevin was the 'King of the Assists' once more, and what an amazing assist it was.

'Wow, okay, you deserve that award!' Leroy admitted graciously.

Kevin had found the perfect finish to an almost perfect season. He had come so far since his difficult days at Chelsea. He was now a Premier League Champion and a League Cup winner with Manchester City, as well as one of the best playmakers in the world.

And yet, Kevin was already hungry for more. He updated his 'to-win' list:

1. The 2018 World Cup with Belgium.
2. The 2019 Champions League with Manchester City.

Turn the page for a sneak preview of
another brilliant football story by
Matt and Tom Oldfield. . .

SALAH

Available now!

CHAPTER 1

EUROPEAN SUPERSTAR

Anfield, 24 April 2018

The atmosphere at Anfield was always amazing but on big European nights, it was extra special. The chorus of the Kop started hours before kick-off and, if Liverpool were to beat Roma, it would go on for days afterwards. The fans sang the old favourites like 'You'll Never Walk Alone', and they sang the new favourites too:

Mo Salah, Mo Salah
Running down the wing,
Salah la la la la la la
Egyptian King!

The eyes of the world were on Liverpool's 'Egyptian

King'. Mohamed was in the best form of his life, with forty goals and counting. He had already scored thirty-one in the Premier League and nine in the Champions League. Could he keep shooting his team all the way to the final?

For Mohamed, it was going to be an emotional night, no matter what. First of all, he was playing in his first-ever Champions League semi-final, a moment that he had dreamed about ever since he was an eight-year-old boy. He was following in the footsteps of his heroes like Zinedine Zidane and Francesco Totti.

Mohamed was also playing against his old club. When his big move to Chelsea hadn't worked out, it was Italian football that saved him. At Fiorentina, and then Roma, he had rediscovered his passion, his confidence, and the path to superstardom. He would always be grateful for that.

Mohamed's old manager, Luciano Spalletti, had moved on, but lots of his old teammates were still there – Radja Nainggolan, Stephan El Shaarawy, and his old strike partner, Edin Džeko. In the tunnel, Mohamed hugged each and every one of them.

'Good luck,' he said with a smile, 'may the best team win!'

Liverpool were far from a one-man team. Mohamed was one part of 'The Big Three', the hottest strikeforce in the world. With Sadio Mané on the left, Roberto Firmino in the middle, and Mohamed on the right, the Reds looked unstoppable. Even Philippe Coutinho's move to Barcelona hadn't slowed them down. They had scored five against Porto in the Round of 16 and then five against Manchester City in the quarter-finals too. If the Roma defenders weren't careful, 'The Big Three' would run riot again.

'Come on lads, let's win this!' the Liverpool captain Jordan Henderson shouted as the players took up their positions for kick-off.

Even during his days at Roma, Mohamed had been more of a winger than a striker. With his amazing sprint speed, he would race past defenders and set up chances for Edin. At Liverpool, however, manager Jürgen Klopp had helped turn Mohamed into a proper forward and a goalscoring machine. He still worked hard for his team but he did it higher up the pitch.

That way, if a defender made a mistake, he was always ready to pounce.

Liverpool created their first good opening after twenty-seven minutes. One clever flick from Roberto was all it took to set speedy Sadio away. He had Mohamed to his right but Sadio wanted the glory for himself. In the penalty area, he pulled back his left foot and... blazed it over the crossbar!

The Liverpool fans buried their heads in their hands – what a missed opportunity! Two minutes later, another one arrived. Mohamed played a great pass to Roberto, who squared it to Sadio. He hit it first time... high and wide!

Groans rang out around Anfield. They couldn't keep wasting these opportunities! Liverpool needed more composure in front of goal. What they needed was a cool head...

Sadio passed to Roberto, who passed to Mohamed on the right side of the box. With a quick tap of the boot, he shifted the ball onto his lethal left foot. Time to shoot? No, not quite yet. Mohamed took one more touch to get a better angle, and then curled a fierce strike into the top corner. The technique was astonishing and he made it look so easy.

Goooooooooooooooooooooaaaaaaaaaaaaaaaaallllllllllllll llllllllllllllll!!!!!!!!!!!!!!!!!!

Mohamed put his arms up straight away – he wasn't going to celebrate a goal against his old team. That didn't stop the Liverpool fans, though, or his new teammates.

'Get in!' Jordan screamed, punching the air.

In the last minute of the first half, Mohamed passed to Roberto near the halfway line and sprinted forward for the one-two. The Roma defenders had no chance of catching him. Instead, their goalkeeper rushed out to the edge of his area to block the shot but Mohamed lifted the ball delicately over him. So calm and so classy! As it rolled into the back of the net, he lifted his arms up again.

Goooooooooooooooooooooaaaaaaaaaaaaaaaaallllllllllllll llllllllllllllll!!!!!!!!!!!!!!!!!!

There was just no stopping Mohamed. In the second half, he beat Roma's offside trap again and crossed to Sadio for a simple tap-in. *3–0!*

They pointed over at Roberto. 'Bobby, it's your turn to score now!'

Mohamed picked the ball up on the right wing and attacked the poor Roma left-back, who backed away in fear. Hadn't Mohamed done enough damage for one day? No! He danced his way through and crossed to Roberto at the back post. *4–0!*

Liverpool's 'Big Three' were all on the scoresheet yet again. It was party time at Anfield:

We've got Salah, do do do do do do!

Mané Mané, do do do do do,

And Bobby Firmino,

And we sold Coutinho!

After seventy-five brilliant minutes, Klopp gave his superstar a well-deserved rest. As Mohamed left the pitch, both sets of fans stood up to clap his world-class performance, and the humble hero clapped right back.

At Basel, Mohamed had become a European star; at Liverpool, he had become a European *super*star. With two great goals and two amazing assists, Mohamed had led Liverpool towards the Champions League final, just as he had led his country, Egypt, to the 2018 World Cup.

'So, just how good *is* Mohamed Salah?' the TV presenter asked.

Liverpool legend Steven Gerrard smiled and replied: 'He's the best player on the planet right now!'

That had always been Mohamed's dream, ever since he first kicked a football on his local pitch in Nagrig.

KEVIN DE BRUYNE HONOURS

Anderlecht
🏆 Belgian Pro League: 2010–11

VfL Wolfsburg
🏆 DFB-Pokal: 2014–15

Manchester City
🏆 Premier League: 2017–18
🏆 Football League/EFL Cup: 2017–18

Individual
🏆 Bundesliga Young Player of the Year: 2012–13
🏆 Bundesliga Player of the Year: 2014–15
🏆 Bundesliga Team of the Year: 2014–15

Belgian Sportsman of the Year: 2015

 Manchester City Player of the Year: 2015–16, 2017–18

 UEFA Team of the Year: 2017

 Premier League Team of the Year: 2017–18

 Premier League Playmaker of the Season: 2017–18

DE BRUYNE

9

THE FACTS

NAME: KEVIN DE BRUYNE

DATE OF BIRTH: 28 June 1991

AGE: 26

PLACE OF BIRTH: Drongen

NATIONALITY: Belgium

BEST FRIEND: Eden Hazard

CURRENT CLUB: Manchester City

POSITION: CAM

THE STATS

Height (cm):	181
Club appearances:	369
Club goals:	82
Club trophies:	4
International appearances:	65
International goals:	14
International trophies:	0
Ballon d'Ors:	0

★ ★ ★ **HERO RATING: 90** ★ ★ ★

GREATEST MOMENTS

Type and search the web links to see the magic for yourself!

⭐ 1 29 OCTOBER 2011, CLUB BRUGGE 4–5 GENK

https://www.youtube.com/watch?v=LBgG28PzQ_M
At the age of twenty, Kevin was already the star of Belgian football. And after winning the 2010–11 First Division title, he just got better and better. This brilliant hat-trick against Club Brugge won the game for Genk and certainly impressed Roman Abramovich. Four months later, Kevin signed for Chelsea for £7 million.

1 JULY 2014, BELGIUM 2–1 USA

https://www.youtube.com/watch?v=r51_9J2Y9-c

With a string of great performances, Kevin forced his way into the Belgium team just in time for the 2014 World Cup in Brazil. In extra time in the Round of 16, Kevin cut past two American defenders and steered his shot past the goalkeeper's outstretched leg. 1–0! Finally, the Red Devils had the breakthrough they needed.

30 JANUARY 2015, VFL WOLFSBURG 4–1 BAYERN MUNICH

https://www.youtube.com/watch?v=Fi9z87Ver1Q

Kevin's midfield masterclasses don't get much better than this thrashing of German Champions, Bayern Munich. He set up the first goal for Bas Dost and then scored two great goals of his own. The Bayern defence just could not cope with his bursting runs. Their manager Pep Guardiola had tried but failed to sign Kevin, but he got his man later at Manchester City.

4 ★ 12 APRIL 2016,
MANCHESTER CITY 1–0 PSG

https://www.youtube.com/watch?v=nHUVInq2E_8

Manchester City returned from Paris with two away goals but they still had a job to do at the Etihad. With fifteen minutes to go, Kevin tricked Edinson Cavani with a drop of the shoulder and then curled an incredible shot past the goalkeeper. 1–0! That strike sent City into the Champions League semi-finals.

5 ★ 30 SEPTEMBER 2017,
CHELSEA 0–1 MANCHESTER CITY

https://www.youtube.com/watch?v=MfHjXmlGJ5s

After a great start to the new season, Manchester City travelled to Kevin's old club, the reigning Premier League Champions, Chelsea. The game was heading for a 0–0 draw until Kevin stepped up with a stunning left-foot strike past his Belgium teammate, Thibaut Courtois. It was another moment of magic from Pep Guardiola's star man and it kept City top of the table.

PLAY LIKE YOUR HEROES

THE KEVIN DE BRUYNE THROUGH-BALL

SEE IT HERE You Tube

https://www.youtube.com/watch?v=Hhmim0_yCSM

STEP 1: Move into space to receive the ball in central midfield. Call for it! Keep looking around you. It's best to plan your next pass before you even get the ball.

STEP 2: When it arrives, play the pass as quickly as possible. The longer you hold on to the ball, the more time the defenders have to get prepared.

STEP 3: Get your angles right! You need the ball to reach your teammate and get past your opponents. It has to be the perfect pass.

STEP 4: Get the power right! Too weak and an opponent might get there first; too strong and your teammate might not be able to control it.

STEP 5: Don't stop to admire your work! Keep running in case there's a chance for a rebound.

TEST YOUR KNOWLEDGE

QUESTIONS

1. Which football team did Kevin support as a child?

2. How old was Kevin when he gave his first TV interviews?

3. How old was Kevin when he moved from Gent to Genk?

4. Who did Kevin form a great attacking partnership with during his time with the Genk Under-21s?

5. How much did Chelsea pay for Kevin?

6. How many Premier League goals did Kevin score for Chelsea?

7. Which two German clubs has Kevin played for?

8. Kevin has won the Bundesliga title – true or false?

9. Kevin scored an important extra-time goal for Belgium at the 2014 World Cup against which country?

10. Which Manchester City manager signed Kevin for £58 million?

11. How many times has Kevin finished top of the Premier League Assists chart?

Answers below. . . No cheating!

1. *Liverpool* 2. *Eleven* 3. *Fourteen* 4. *Christian Benteke* 5. *£7 million*
6. *None* 7. *Werder Bremen and VfL Wolfsburg* 8. *False – although Wolfsburg were runners-up in the 2014–15 season, and they did win the German Cup!* 9. *The USA* 10. *Manuel Pellegrini* 11. *Twice – in 2016–17 (eighteen assists) and 2017–18 (sixteen assists)*

HAVE YOU GOT THEM ALL?

FOOTBALL HEROES